SUZANNE COLLINS
THE HUNGER GAMESMAKER

NY Times Best-seller
MARC SHAPIRO

Suzanne Collins: The Hunger GamesMaker©2025 by Marc Shapiro

All Rights Reserved. No part of this book may be reproduced or transmitted in any form or by any means, electronic or mechanical, including photocopying, without permission in writing from the publisher.

This publisher does not allow any part of this book to be used or reproduced in any manner to train artificial intelligence technologies or systems.

For more information contact:
Riverdale Avenue Books
5676 Riverdale Avenue
Riverdale, NY 10471.

www.riverdaleavebooks.com
Design by www.formatting4U.com
Cover Design by Scott Carpenter

Digital ISBN: 978162601708
Print ISBN: 9781626017122

First Edition: March 2025

This Book Is Dedicated To…

Imagination.
Imagination is a gift from the Gods. To use imagination to create is a blessing. To experience the fruits of an imaginative mind is a privilege. Imagination takes us out of the hum drum realities of life. In the best possible way, imagination is an escape to be savored.

TABLE OF CONTENTS

PROLOGUE Okay How Does It Feel? i
INTRODUCTION How Does She Do It? 1
ONE Meet the Folks 7
TWO Military Brat 9
THREE Indiana Wants Suzanne 13
FOUR Suzanne Bites the Big Apple 17
FIVE A Family Way 21
SIX Suzanne Wrote the Book 23
SEVEN With Time On Her Hands 29
EIGHT Anatomy of a Best Seller 31
NINE Let the Games Begin 33
TEN The Fame Game 39
ELEVEN Which Came First? 41
TWELVE Write the Sequel Yesterday 45
THIRTEEN Agree to Disagree 49
FOURTEEN Lights, Camera, The Back Story 53
FIFTEEN An Enormously Tricky Thing To Do 57
SIXTEEN Welcome to the Jungle 61
SEVENTEEN Hollywood Catches Fire 67
EIGHTEEN The Ex… Or Are They? 71
NINETEEN Was Two Mockingjays Too Much? 75
TWENTY Okay What's Next? 79
TWENTY-ONE Who Owns The Hunger? 81
TWENTY-TWO When In Doubt… Songbirds and Snakes ... 85
TWENTY-THREE Songbirds and Snakes: The Movie 89
TWENTY-FOUR Hunger Raises the Curtain 91

TWENTY-FIVE The Reaping Keeps Hunger Alive 93
TWENTY-SIX I'm Very Excited..97
TWENTY-SEVEN Living the Hunger Games Life 101
TWENTY-EIGHT In Her Own Words 105
ADDENDUM: How The Films Were Made...........................109
APPENDIX 121
SOURCES..129
ABOUT THE AUTHOR...131

PROLOGUE
Okay How Does It Feel?

There are different levels of questioning, especially when it comes to the probing of a rising literary light. J.K. Rowling most likely has heard the questions a million times. Stephenie Meyer has certainly heard them more times than she can count.

There's the technical stuff, the nuts and bolts stuff. But at the end of the day, it's the questions that strike at the essence of person and craft and humanity that ring truest to a creative mind. The later was definitely in play in 2013 when the reporter for *Time Magazine* asked by this time the notoriously press-shy Suzanne Collins just how it feels to be the next big thing. Collins most likely had to think about it a moment. But her response was simple, even and struck at the essence of the person behind the mega success.

"My real life hasn't changed much. I mean I still have the same friends and my family, my life and my writing. The big change would be that this is the first time in my career where I've been able to work on whatever I wanted and not have financial concerns involved."

For Suzanne Collins, how it felt meant one important thing. It meant being free.

INTRODUCTION
How Does She Do It?

Okay. So how does Suzanne Collins do it?

J.K. Rowling gets asked that question a lot.. And I'm sure it is the question that Rebecca Yarros is asked almost every day.

It is a question that defies genre even though, in all candor, it is often addressed to the currently in vogue perception of the rise of female authors in the arena of often bleak and fantastical dystopian science fiction and fantasy. That the question gets asked at all is a sign that we have arrived at a place where people just want to know.

And when your books have sold more than a 100,000,000 copies, have been adapted into movies that have brought everyone who has read the books into the theaters and your bank balance for 2024 was estimated at north of $80 million…

Well, people just want an insight into the magic bullet.

In an early conversation with *Scholastic Magazine*, Collins kind of, sort of answered the question when she offered that her workday began with a snap, crackle and pop.

"I grab some cereal and sit down to work as soon as possible. The more distractions I have to deal with before I begin writing, the harder focusing on the story becomes.

Then I work until I'm tapped out. Usually somewhere in the early afternoon. If I actually write three to five hours that's a productive day for me. Some days all I do is stare at the wall. That can be productive too."

And on other days, she laughingly recalled in a quote from *The Writing Cooperative.com*, "I wrote *The Hunger Games* in a chair, like a *Lazy Boy* chair next to my bed. I had an office but my kids sort of took that over."

As it turns out, the normally press-shy Collins seemed to have a soft spot for shop talk and the care and feeding of what she does. She was particularly open when offering up writing tips in conversation with *Living Writer.com* when she shared five distinct tips on how she does what she does.

She starts work in the morning. "It's a simple routine. Eat, then write. By jumping right into work I get rid of possible distractions that may stop me from even starting to write."

Write what you know. "Familiarity allows one to have a lot of information to draw from."

Write what you love. "That is especially applicable when what you know and what you love may not always be the same thing. Passion and excitement easily spill into your work when you write things you love."

Pick your topic first and your audience comes second. "Contextualizing the 'just war theory' into the world of adolescents was the key to the conception of *The Hunger Games* series. I managed to insert a great deal of story that revolves around personal relationships which were more relevant to young adults."

And finally, all stories are made the same way. "You need to tell a good story and you've got to have good characters."

Suzanne Collins, The Hunger GamesMaker

Like all good writers, Collins is particular when it comes to creating her world and waxes quasi philosophical when offering up the nuts and bolts of the care and feeding of *The Hunger Games* universe in conversation with *The New York Times*. "I used to write longhand but now it's all laptop. Definitely not music. Music demands to be listened to. I like quiet but not silence."

And as she would easily expound in a Scholastic interview, she was very big on detail. "Structure is one of my favorite parts of writing. I always work a story out with Post -It notes, sometimes using a different color for a different character arc. I create a chapter grid as well and keep files for later books so that whenever I have an idea for a later book that might be useful I can make a note of it."

Collins has also offered that once a first draft of a completed manuscript is completed, the initial editing process begins at home. "My husband, Cap, and my agent, Rosemary, have consistently been a book's first readers. They both have excellent critical skills and give insightful notes. I like to keep the editorial team as much in the dark as possible so that when they read the first draft it is with completely fresh eyes."

But once she found the time and space to actually sit down and tell the tale, Collins' ability as a master storyteller, coupled with all manner of influences that included such young adult staples as action, drama, romance, a bit of horror and violence and a healthy mixture of Greek mythology and a believable, real world attitude about war and its consequences into a futuristic, dystopian nightmare in which class warfare and its real world counterpart form a believable juxtaposition of fact and fantasy and a natural growth of a readership that was getting older and, to a certain degree, outgrowing the efforts of J.K. Rowling and Stephenie Meyer.

During her writing of *The Hunger Games* series, Collins can go on forever exploring the research and intricacies of the futuristic world and how it operates. But, in true writerly insight and passion, she always returns, as she offers in *The New York Times*, to the core of her stories, the characters. "I definitely do picture the characters as I'm writing them. For me, the characters are like a 'basket of diamonds to me, revolving around stories that are made to be shared."

But behind all the creative talk about literature and war and anti- war messaging, *The Hunger Games* and its creator had also entered the realm of pop culture and a sense of corporate reality, bottom lines and the potential in both book and movie form of sequels, spin offs and all manner of squeezing blood out of the proverbial turnip.

The last *Hunger Games* book came out in 2020 (although the last movie was released in 2023) nearly five years in the rear view mirror. Book publishers and movie studios were getting anxious. They wanted what they wanted but Collins could not be rushed, especially since she perceived *The Hunger Games* as finite as she reflected in *The Writing Cooperative.com.*

"*The Hunger Games* right now is getting a lot of focus. But it will pass. Then the focus will be on something else. It'll shift. It always does. And that seems just fine."

But in the meantime, there would be more *The Hunger Games* on the horizon. On June 6, 2024, outlets as diverse as *AP News*, *USA Today* and *Scholastic* publications excitedly proclaimed that *The Sunrise on the Reaping* was now set for release on March 18, 2025. *The Sunrise on the Reaping*, a prequel set 24 years before the original Hunger Games chronology and centered around the 50th Hunger Games battles which had been won by Haymitch Abernathy. Lionsgate Films almost immediately announced that the film version of the prequel would be released midway through 2026.

Collins, who is media savvy but at the same time publicity shy, hates having her picture taken, will rarely do interviews except for those doled out by her publisher, is, for the most part, just plain folks and down home. She would just as soon read a book, watch some television or deal with the everyday challenges of being a wife and mother than pontificate on all the real and imagined nuances of what she has created. Her drive for anonymity amidst the stardom that her books and, subsequent movies, has brought her is palpable. Truth be known, Suzanne Collins would just as soon be left alone to do what it is she does in peace.

For the most part, she has come to recognize the impact and importance of the new book and movie and as a high-water mark on a career that had no signs of letting up. Still she was a bit reserved in sharing about where the story she had created was heading, in a quote from *USA Today*. "The book will offer a deeper dive into the use of propaganda and the power of those who control the narrative. The question of real or not real seems more to me every-day."

The Hunger Gamesmaker is not the endless expected episode guide that inevitably follows the rise to pop culture greatness with the mind-numbing episode guides that are preaching to the fandom of a particular entity who already, in Collins' case, have read the books countless times, seen the movies countless times and who could have written the verbatim pages of plot and character listings themselves.

While there is the all-important biographical stuff,

this book does a deeper dive than names, dates and places. It delves into the psychology of the creator, the state of mind when the magic happened, how their creation impacts pop culture, the dollars and cents of what one manifests in their heart and soul, the tenor of the times and the philosophy, often controversial and quite worthy approach of the shy, quiet author and her outlook on childhood, war and violence that is at the center piece of her creation.

This is where Suzanne Collins is now. What follows is how she got here and what was in her head.

CHAPTER ONE
Meet the Folks

One thing has been certain. When America has gone to war, a Collins was there to pick up a gun and join the fight.

World War I saw Suzanne's grandfather doubled over after being gassed by enemy fire. World War II saw an uncle pelted with enemy bullets for which he received several shrapnel wounds. That Michael John Collins ended up continuing the family tradition of fighting for his country came as no surprise.

Going to war was in the Collins' family genes. And when the Korean conflict got underway, it was not long before Collins, newly married to Jane Brady Collins, was the latest member of the Collins family tree to join the fight.

For his part, Collins quickly carved out a notable record as an air force pilot in the Korean War before, years later, serving a tour of duty in Vietnam, earning both the Distinguished Flying Cross and the Bronze Star for heroism. In later years, Collins brought his military know-how and dedication to the service with postings to NATO and the Pentagon.

Collins' sense of military might and the deeper concepts of war most likely were born growing up in The Great Depression when, according to a *World Press.com* account, his family would often go into the woods with their guns, not for sport but, rather, to put food on the table.

Collins' impressions of her parents relationship has been reported in bits and pieces, small moments and impressions that often seemed literary in their simplicity and detail as she remembered in *A-Z Quotes.com* and *Scholastic Press.com*. "When I think of my parents, I think of the way my father never failed to bring my mother gifts when he would go into the woods and that my mother's face would light up at the sound of his boots at the door."

Of her father, Collins' impressions were seemingly more to the point and, by degrees, practical but no less admiring as she related in *Mederia 7.com Weebly*. "My father was career Air Force and also a Vietnam veteran. Beyond that he was also a Doctor of Political Science. He was a military specialist who was very well educated. It was very important to him that we understand things because of what he did and what he experienced."

Her father's roots also came up in *World Press.com* when she offered an early assessment of just where much of her creative insights came from. "My father had a gift for presenting history as a fascinating story."

The Collins' family was stepped in tradition, conservative values and, as it turned out, a feeling for history and its telling. By the mid 50's they began to meet their ideal of a large family with the birth of Kathryn (born 1957), Andrew (born 1958) and Joan (born 1960). Suzanne Collins was born on August 10, 1962 in Hartford, Connecticut.

The life, journey and adventure had just begun.

CHAPTER TWO
Military Brat

As far back as she could remember, Collins was up close with the long-held tag of what military family members called the Military Brat.

"When I was growing up, we moved all the time because my dad was in the Air Force," she reflected in a *Scholastic Press* interview. We were mostly in the eastern part of the United States and in Europe and we were always moving. I definitely knew what it was like to be a stranger somewhere."

In the same conversation, Collins remembered that the price she paid for being the youngest child in a family of four children soon became obvious. "I had two older sisters and an older brother and I hold them responsible for the trouble I got into growing up. I believe that being the youngest child, that was my right."

But through the unexpected twists and turns of being a Military Brat, Collins managed to get along, developing interests in gymnastics, reading and often running in the woods with friends, albeit temporary, that she managed to make wherever they were. From the outset, there was a sense of fantasy and discovery in Collins, traits that seemed to be reinforced and confirmed in her psyche at every turn and, as she confirmed at a fairly early age in *Weebly.com*.

"In the fifth and sixth grade, I went to school in an open classroom and the English teacher, Miss Vance, was wonderful. On the rainy days, she would take whoever was interested to the side and read us Edgar Allan Poe stories. I remember all of us sitting wide-eyed as she read *'The Tell Tale Heart'* or *'The Mask of the Red Death.'* She didn't think that we were too young to hear it and we were riveted. Those stories made a huge impression on me. Those stories were about death, loss and violence. But I think, if accepted the right way, kids will accept any number of things."

A voracious reader at a very early age, Collins would expand her reading library to such titles as *A Wrinkle in Time* by Madeline L Engle, *The Phantom Tollbooth* by Norton Juster and Jules Feiffer, *A Tree Grows in Brooklyn* by Betty Smith and, perhaps most telling, *1984* by George Orwell.

Collins' childhood education to the darker realities of life continued in 1968 when, at age six, the family relocated to Indiana and Collins' father was subsequently deployed to Vietnam for a year. As she explored in *Culturus Magazine*, *The New York Times* and *Brainy Quotes.com*, Collin's childhood apprehension about war and conflict grew as did her understanding of war and violence as only a child could perceive it.

"If your parent is deployed and you are young, you spend the whole time wondering where they are and wanting them to come home. As time passes and the absence is longer and longer, you become more and more concerned. But you don't really have the words to express your concern. There's only the continued absence."

Collins' mother, Jane ,would do her best to calm her family's unease during her husband's absence. Collins, in *Brainy Quotes.com* was to reflect on those efforts.

Suzanne Collins, The Hunger GamesMaker

"My mother tried really hard to protect us but occasionally, after afternoon cartoons or whatever was on, the nightly news would come on with footage and news reports of the Vietnam war zone and I would hear the word Vietnam and I know that my dad was over there and it was a very frightening experience for me."

Collins' father returned from active duty in Vietnam in 1969, physically unharmed but emotionally and mentally changed. There were scars, nightmares and, because of his nature to educate his children about the reality of war, his daughter would hear quite a bit.

CHAPTER THREE
Indiana Wants Suzanne

The Collins family would spend the next few years hopscotching between the Southern part of the United States and Europe.

Wherever they went, the family would inevitably tour military monuments and historical battle sights where Collins and her siblings received their father's military background and experience up close and personal. It was not uncommon during more touristy oriented tours that Collins and her father would often lag behind during which her father would promptly fill in historical background to the concept of history and war that the tour guides soft peddled. And Collins' father did not pull any punches.

Collins would recall those moments in a *Biography.com* entry.

"I believe my father felt a great responsibility and urgency about educating his children about war. He would frequently take us to places like battlefields and war monuments. He would talk about whatever precipitated the war and moved up through the battlefield we were standing in. It was a great tour guide experience. Throughout our lives we basically heard about war."

Although quite young, nevertheless the young girl looked at her father's war stories with the eye of a creative as she explored in *Examiner.com*. "He had a gift for presenting history as a fascinating story. He also seemed to have a good sense of exactly how much a child could handle which is quite a bit."

Often overshadowed but duly noted in *Book Analysis.com* was the early influence Collins' mother Jane, a history teacher with a penchant for great literature that took in everything regardless of genre, had on her daughter. Collins was introduced to the wonders of science fiction and fantasy as well as what Greek and Roman mythology had to offer and, in hindsight would guide her in her early approach to writing.

The Collins family would eventually set down some semblance of roots in the late 1970's in Birmingham, Alabama where Collins would, subsequently be enrolled in the Alabama School of Fine Arts as a Theater Arts Major. Due in large part to the notion that, at an early age, the young child was of a creative mindset.

Collins had, beginning at age 12, decided that she was going to act. She had a sense of being out on stage and creating characters as something that she would, quite simply, like to do. Her time at Alabama School of Fine Arts is noted in fragments. Time dutifully chronicled that Collins took archery classes in gym class.

In a rare expressive moment of those times, *Puget Sound.com* reported that Collins acknowledged a creative writing class, reportedly her first formal education in the writing arts. "If there is one rule of writing that has stuck with me from my high school creative writing class it was show don't tell."

Collins graduated from the Alabama School of Fine Arts at age 18 with a degree in Theater Arts. But she was not finished with higher education. She would soon matriculate to even higher education at Indiana State University in 1985 doing double duty on a Bachelor's Degree program that included two majors, Theater and Telecommunications as chronicled by the *Indiana Daily Student newspaper.*

Collins' stay at IU was a time of growth in which she saw the potential of growth and creative expression. She was flexing her acting muscles on occasion, specifically in a university theater production of the thriller *Forest Gates* in which her multi- faceted approach to nuance and character in the context of a theater production some observed was well beyond her years. The play's author, Steve Timm said as much in conversation with De Pauw University.edu when he offered "You knew she clearly had a lot of talent and she fit exactly what we were trying to do."

It would be almost an afterthought that, along the way, Collins would meet fellow cast member Charles 'Cap' Pryor. They got a long on a social level, occasionally hanging out together. But like just about every aspect of Collins' quest for privacy, if there was anything going on beyond that, it was never confirmed or certain.

By the time Collins had reached her final year at Indiana University, her creative goals were beginning to evolve. To that point, she had continued to remain very much an actress. But that changed by the time she turned 20 as she remembered in *Finding Dulicinca.com*. "Around that time I got the idea that I didn't just want to speak the words. I wanted to write them as well."

Collins would graduate from Indiana University in 1985 with a Bachelor's Degree in both of her majors, Theater and Telecommunications. But the aura of accomplishment was almost immediately replaced by the reality of having to pay the bills.

How Collins dealt with that reality was offered in a *Brainy Quotes.com* extract and *The Sydney Morning Herald*.

"When I got out of undergrad (*Indiana University*), I had this degree in theater and telecommunications. My first job? I was a news reporter for the local stories for National Public Radio. Then I was a country and western DJ. Then I did data entry for a year book company. By that time I was in my mid 20's. I decided to go to grad school.

"I decided to specialize in playwriting."

CHAPTER FOUR
Suzanne Bites the Big Apple

New York University's Tisch School of the Arts had much that appealed to Collins' spirit of excitement and creative electricity.

For openers, NYU was legendary for being the starting point for boatloads of future super star quality talent. Among those who spent time learning the ropes at NYU were Alec Baldwin (actor), Chris Columbus (director), Clive Davis (record producer), Neil Diamond (singer), Spike Lee (director), Lady Gaga (singer) and John Waters (director). This was certainly the place where Collins wanted to be.

In 1989, Collins entered NYU, putting the notion of becoming an actress to the side in favor of an ambitious four year journey towards a Masters Degree in Dramatic Writing. Given her nomadic background, Collins adjusted quite easily to the hustle and bustle that was the NYU creative scene, experiencing all that the Big Apple had to offer while proving quite adept at learning the techniques, story structure and characterization of writing for the big and small screen.

But making new friends and having new experiences did not prevent her from keeping in touch with her old Indiana buddy Charlie 'Cap' Pryor who by the early 90's had also made his way to New York and was attempting to make it as an actor.

Marc Shapiro

Reports on the particulars of how they got together romantically, just like just about every aspect of Collins' personal life, tend to differ. Some reports indicate they were together romantically as early as 1990 while the more popular theory was that they were officially a couple in 1991 and would marry in 1992.

With her personal/romantic life seemingly in order, Collins would graduate from *NYU* the same year she married. The couple were living a sparse, semi-bohemian existence during that first year but for Collins, her freshly minted Dramatic Writing Masters Degree in tow, was soon on the job market.

She would not be unemployed for long. In fact, before she graduated from NYU, Collins resume found its way to the Nickelodeon children's television conglomerate who hired the recent grad as a writer on such shows as *Clarissa Explains It All*, *The Mystery Files of Shelby Woo*, *Little Bear and Oswald* and *The Wow! Wow! Wubbzy*. Word eventually got across town to PBS who hired Collins as head writer on their show *Clifford's Puppy Days*.

At one point, Collins, as excerpted in *Brainy Quotes*, had a good laugh at her success. "I have a pretty big television background. I've clocked so many hours in so many writer's rooms over the years."

She would also acknowledge that for a person who loved isolation, the television writing left a bit to be desired. "Writing for television is very collaborative and relatively anonymous. Since there are so many writers involved there's not much attention paid to an individual writer."

But while, admittedly, her plans were to pen more adult fare, she put up a spirited defense of her children's output in *Mediaroom. Scholastic.com*. "I started out as a playwright for adult audiences. When the television work

Suzanne Collins, The Hunger GamesMaker

came along, it was primarily for children. But, whatever age you're writing for, the same rules of plot, character and theme apply. You just set up a world and try to remain true to it."

CHAPTER FIVE
A Family Way

Collins and her husband were living what would be the idyllic New York City life. They were in love in the big city and doing their best to make a go of it in the creative life.

She was quickly becoming the go-to writer on just about every one of Nickelodeon's children's television shows. Charles was slowly but surely finding his way with bit parts as an actor and as a teacher of special needs children. There were countless sights and sounds to experience. Up until the early 90's, this was where they wanted to live and work.

"We lived in New York City a long time," she offered in *Book Page.com*. "It was a great place to live and work."

But by the early 90's, the couple felt it was time for a change. It was time to have children. The couple's first child, a boy named Charlie, was born in 1994. Five years later a second child, a girl named Isabelle, was born in 1999. With the coming of a second child, things began to get a bit cramped in an apartment that had been ideal for two as Collins reported in *Book Page.com*. "With two children, we were bursting out of the apartment." Consequently, and quite logically, it was determined that it would be next to impossible to find a place suitable for two adults and two children that they could afford, and so the couple made the decision to move to Sandy Hook, Connecticut.

For Collins, it was a return to home. Besides being her birth place, Collins and Pryor lived in the Sandy Hook area before they were married and it was where a number of Pryor's family and friends resided. It was duly noted in a 2016 *Warsaw Times Union* article that she became the darling of the area, largely due to her non-Hollywood ways as reported by Laurie Owen, an area resident and Dean of the School of Education.

"When the families get together, they just talk about family matters. Charles and Suzanne are just the kindest, most humble people. They are far removed from Hollywood. Suzanne's image in the public is very much her. She is very quiet and introverted. She's the same person she's always been. Anyone who knows her knows that success will not change her as a person."

However, as the years went by and the children got older, the difference in the couple's income brought Charles and Suzanne to make the quite logical decision for Charles to devote all his time and energy into being the caretaker of the children's day to day upbringing so that Suzanne could concentrate on her work. Dixie Pryor, Charles' mother, would put a positive spin on the decision in the *Warsaw Times Union*.

"Cap still does a little bit of acting but now he is predominantly the caretaker of the children. He did teach for a few years but he gave that up to take care of his kids."

CHAPTER SIX
Suzanne Wrote the Book

Generation O!. If you blinked you may have missed it. One season, 13 half hour episodes (2000-2001), a spirited bit of animation that had the distinction of featuring a song and dance number in each episode.

For Suzanne Collins, *Generation O!* would be a pivotal moment in her life and career.

Prior to *Generation O!,* Collins had taken a tentative first step toward actually writing a book with 1999's rarely acknowledged novelization spin-off of *The Mystery Files of Shelby Woo* which Collins wrote, *Fire Proof: Shelby Woo #11*. For completists, this would be Collins' very first book.

Fire Proof was a good first exercise in book writing for Collins. The book mirrored the television show format, a simple tale of childlike mystery and suspense aimed directly at a nine to 12-year-olds. In the novel, Shelby Woo and her friends Vince and Angie are in London as part of a student cultural exchange program when they stumble upon a strange case of arson during a theater production of *Romeo & Juliet*. The story was fairly formulaic but allowed Collins to step away from a television writing form and play with character and story structure in a book form. As a book author it was a learning experience and a good first step.

James Proimos was a creative jack of all trades,

author, illustrator and, in the case of *Generation O!*, co-creator. Consequently, he had an eye for talent and he knew almost immediately that Collins knew how to tell a story. During writing room chats and lunch breaks, Collins would often entertain Proimos with story ideas. And just as often, Proimos would ask "why don't you write a book?"

Proimos would recall his encouragement and enthusiasm in *Deseret News*. "She seemed like a book writer to me. It was sort of her personality. She also had the style and mind of a novelist. I was telling her that you can do television forever because it's a young person's business. With books, at the very worst, you start out slow but you can do books for the rest of your life"

Finally, Collins took the hint as she disclosed in *Newsweek*. "The Gregor books were very much what I would call lightning bolt ideas. There was just this moment when the ideas came to me."

Best described as *Alice in Wonderland* mixed in with subtle shades of political and militaristic, *Gregor the Overlander* follows the epic fantasy tale of Gregor and his sister Boots who fall through a vent in their apartment basement and find themselves in a world called the *Underland* which is inhabited by pale human beings and giant animals and shaded with societal, political and militaristic elements. Needless to say, with her background in creating children's television, it did not come as a surprise that *Gregor the Overlander* was aimed at a young adult audience.

Collins reflected as much in *Suzanne Collins Books.com.*

"I liked the fact that this world was teeming under New York City and nobody was aware of it. That you could be going along, preoccupied with your own problems and then, all of a sudden, whoosh! You take a wrong turn in your laundry room and suddenly a giant cockroach is in your face. No magic. No space or time travel. There's just a ticket to another world right behind your clothes dryer."

Gregor the Overlander would find a willing publisher with *Scholastic* at a time when the new wave of young adult literature was coming into its own. The book would be a commercial and critical success.

School Library Journal wrote, "The book is an engrossing adventure for fantasy fans and for those new to the genre." *Common Sense Media* review stated that "the book's strong characters, vivid descriptions, flawless pacing, breathless excitement, laughs, scares and a vision that makes the fantasy very different." *Publisher's Weekly* praised the book when it said "Collins does a grand job of world building."

And one thing was for certain.

With the success of the first book, there would be an almost immediate demand, both from the public and the publisher, for what happens next. Collins, flushed and appreciative to the response of *Gregor the Overlander*, readily agreed to a follow up in the Gregor saga.

There would be more to come.

Between 2003 and 2007, Collins would write and publish four more books in the *Overlander* series, *Gregor and the Prophecy of Bane*, *Gregor and the Curse of the Warmbloods*, *Gregor and the Marks of Secret* and *Gregor and the Code of Claw*. The series would be edited by Kate Eagan, a solid professional who guided with a subtle and knowing hand Collins' first sustained literary works.

In an interview with the *Sarah Lawrence Blog*, Eagan, discussed Collins' approach to the *Gregor/Undeland* series.

"*The Underland Chronicles* are meant for a younger

audience but share a central theme. Suzanne's main interest is the question of just what is a just war? She is especially concerned about the effects of war on a person."

The author/editor relationship between Collins and Eagan was a smooth one. Eagan offering up the occasional suggestion that would strengthen a scene or a character sequence but the editor's job on the *Underland books*, as she explored in the Sarah Lawrence Blog, was made easy. "Suzanne has this un put downable quality to her writing. She knows how to move a story along and to hold a kid's attention."

Collins would draw on her entire bag of literary tricks, her playwright education in NYU as well as the on-the-job education of structure, pacing, character and tone that she learned in the television cartoon world. She would also draw heavily on the stories she learned at the feet of her father, especially when it came to transforming real world war stories into a palatable for young adult readers (ages nine to 12) for which the *Overlander* books were intended. Collins would defend her approach in conversation with *Newsweek*.

"I like to take topics like war and introduce them to kids at an early age. If you look at the *Gregor* books, they have all kinds of topics. There's biological warfare, there's genocide and there's military intelligence. But it's a fantasy. It's played out with a combination of humans, bats and rats. I want kids to be aware of these topics, to think about them and really, the sooner the better."

In the same *Newsweek* conversation, Collins said that the length and depth of the *Gregor* books inherently required nothing less than a series of books.

"The stories in the *Gregor* books are larger. They

require a series format. If I had written *Gregor* as one book, it would have been 1700 pages. And for a nine to 12-year-old audience that would have been daunting."

By the time Collins had completed the final book in *The Underland Chronicles*, the author, in a *New York Times* interview, said that she was already looking elsewhere. "My brain was already shifting to whatever the next project would be. For the next project I knew I wanted a completely different world and a different angle."

CHAPTER SEVEN
With Time On Her Hands

By 2005, Collins easily had more work then she could handle.

The *Gregor* series alone had reached a pivotal point that was occupying most of her attention and, according to reports, she was still doing occasional television work. But with literally no free moments, she would opt for yet another project, a slight bit of business but a book all the same.

When Charlie McButton Lost Power did have its attraction. A story told completely in rhyme and featuring illustrations geared, in a way, to an even younger age group than the *Gregor* books. In a sense it was a step backward as well as a step forward. It would nevertheless prove a satisfying diversion. And given Collins' tendency to layer her stories with messages and morals, it was spot on.

Long story short, Charlie McButton was a techno whiz. He lived and breathed technology. And so, when an unexpected storm knocked out his source of power, the techno obsessed Charlie was thrown into a literal panic. He needed batteries and the only batteries were in his little sister's talking doll. Charlie would steal the batteries when his sister wasn't around which threw his household into turmoil. Charlie ultimately confessed to the crime which led to his sister and he making peace as only small children do. By playing games the old fashioned way.

Although ultimately becoming an after-thought in the wake of what was to come, *When Charlie McButton Lost His Power* is notable as a small yet effective exercise that showed Collins as somebody with the ability to burn the creative candle at more than one end.

CHAPTER EIGHT
Anatomy of a Best Seller

Literary agent Rosemary Stimola was not too surprised when Collins' pitch for *The Hunger Games* came across her computer screen. After all, she had piloted the author's previous series *The Underland Chronicles* to what was ultimately an international best seller of some note. But even Stimola, in an excerpt from a *Pop Culture Publishing Media Panel*, admitted to doing a mental double take.

Stimola admitted that if any other author had approached her with the idea of a book in which a group of children cast adrift in a dystopian society battle to the death, she might have hesitated. But having already worked with Collins on *The Underland Chronicles*, she knew full well the wealth of information that Collins typically brought to a project as well as her ability to create complex worlds and characters.

Stimola was sold, taking *The Hunger Games* concept under her wing and marching it straight over to *Scholastic Press* who had made a veritable killing when they published *The Underland Chronicles* and would subsequently make a deal for *The Hunger Games* series on the strength of a four-page proposal from Collins.

In a *Book Page.com*, another editor David Levithan offered up the care and feeding of Collins' manuscripts as they came through the editorial door. "When the first drafts of the trilogy came in, it was a little clear who Suzanne felt had the greater claim on Katniss' heart. So, to make it more of a fair fight, I argued a lot for Gale. At some point, Suzanne told me, 'Oh you're Team Gale.' Editorially I am by nature a thinker. But I knew not to try and tinker with Suzanne's story structure."

But as everybody connected to *Scholastic*, and who had discovered in guiding the fortunes of *The Underland Chronicles*, knew there was the author's shy and retiring personality to contend with as well as the creative side to the author.

Especially when it came to the matter of Collins being extremely press shy. Collins' readings and rare public appearances are not to be filmed. She has an extremely low key web presence. In fact on her own modest website Collins made it clear that "I am not on any social media platforms so any accounts that you find in my name are not authorized by me."

To a large extent any interviews were to be 'canned' *Scholastic* handouts and a never ending stream of positive and breathless press announcements. When circumstances dictate that she actually do a non-*Scholastic* controlled interview, she was to be accompanied by a trusted *Scholastic* representative or, for comforts sake, the interviews themselves were to be closely monitored and controlled. Most telling from the moment she signed *The Hunger Games'* deal was that there would be no movie deals made until all the books in *The Hunger Games* series were completed to avoid any undue influences on her writing.

With all the personal guard rails in place, Collins signed on the dotted line and, as she was quoted in *Publishers Weekly*, "I'm blocking out as much as I can."

CHAPTER NINE
Let the Games Begin

The year was 2008.

The last book in *The Underlander* series was just hitting bookshelves. Collins reluctantly was being a good sport about doing as much press as she could tolerate. When the dust finally settled, it was time to creatively and emotionally decompress.

"I was very tired," she recalled in a *Scholastic Video* Interview. "One night I was channel surfing, flipping through images of reality television where these young people were competing for a million dollars or whatever. Then I changed the channel and I was seeing footage from the Iraq war. These two things began to fuse together in a very unsettling way."

And in that moment *The Hunger Games* was born.

"I knew I wanted to continue to explore what I felt was the just war theory for young audiences," she said in *The New York Times*. In *The Underlander Chronicles* I examined the idea of an unjust war because of greed, xenophobia and longstanding hatreds. With *The Hunger Games* I was looking for something different."

But not without doing double duty as she remembered in a *School Library Journal* interview.

"I had been freelancing on a show called *Wow! Wow!*

Wubbsy!. It was a very fun preschool show set in an imaginary town called *Wuzzleburg*. When I was working on *The Hunger* Games, there was not a lot of levity in it. When I would do a *Wubbzy* script, it was an enormous relief to spend some time in *Wuzzleburg*, writing an 11-minute episode where I knew things were going to turn out just fine and all the characters would be alive at the end of the program.'

Which was anything but the case as Collins delved deeper into *The Hunger Games*.

The first book, *The Hunger Games*, was written from the perspective of 16 year-old heroine Katniss Everdeen who lives in the futuristic, post-apocalyptic nation of *Panem* in what passes for life in North America. Society was ruled by *The Capitol*, a highly advanced metropolis that exercises absolute, dictatorial control over the rest of the nation through the use of an annual event called *The Hunger Games* in which one boy and girl, ages 12 to18, from each of the 12 districts surrounding *The Capitol* are selected by lottery to compete in a televised battle to the death.

The process for the first *The Hunger Games,* which would evolve in the subsequent books jelled fairly quickly based on Collins' long held Greek Mythology theme of 'bread and circuses' approach to control the masses. Her fascination with spartan/gladiator movies and Mary Renault's book *The King Must Die*, with its center piece of death and violence as entertainment. Central to Collins' war and control elements would be the time- honored Greek mythology tale of Theseus and the labyrinth as she outlined in *The New York Times*.

"I was such a Greek mythology geek as a kid. It was impossible not to have it come into play in my storytelling.

Suzanne Collins, The Hunger GamesMaker

It was especially true in the story of Theseus in which seven boys and seven girls are chosen by lottery to be thrown into the labyrinth to be destroyed by the Minotaur. I would never go back to thinking of the labyrinth as simply a maze. It will always be an arena to me."

Kate Eagan was familiar with Collins' work, having assisted in bringing *The Underland Chronicles* to completion. Consequently, the editor had a good idea of where *The Hunger Games* and subsequent books in the series were heading as she offered in the Sarah Laurence Blog.

"Storytelling is Suzanne's strength. As an editor, I helped her develop the characters. For example, I asked her for more of the Peta/Katniss/Gale love triangle. Suzanne was more focused on the war story. We learned to trust each other. Sometimes Suzanne thinks it's obvious where she's going. But I'll tell her that I don't see it. When I need help following, it's a sign that the manuscript needs some shoring up."

One thing that Collins discovered while writing *The Hunger Games* was that the often violent and dire elements of the book was that the process could be emotionally taxing to the author's often sympathetic sensibilities.

"When you're writing a story like *The Hunger Games* you have to accept from the beginning that you're going to kill characters," she said in *School Library Journal*. "It's a horrible thing to do and a horrible thing to write. Particularly when you have to take out a character who is vulnerable, young or a character that you have grown to love."

But as she completed the final chapters of *The Hunger Games*, Collins had found herself quite naturally morphing into a wise, if not hardened, defender of the notion of childlike innocence and the concept of war as she offered to *Time Magazine*.

"*The Hunger Games* is part of a larger goal I have which is to write a war appropriate story for every age of kids. I think we put our children at an enormous disadvantage by not educating them in the concept of war, by letting them understand it from a very early age."

As she was well into writing the second book, *Catching Fire*, Collins was also coming to grips with an aspect of the publishing game she had not encountered before.

Don't say a word.

Scholastic Press, in an attempt to generate interest with *The Hunger Games*, went full bore on the hype. Which, in the case of *The Hunger Games*, meant a full-blown embargo on any review copies going out before the actual publication date and, in the case of Collins, in a conversation with *School Library Journal* done a month before the release of the book, made the secrecy just about the only topic the author would talk about.

"There's a lot I have not been able to discuss about the book because it would tip off too much of the ending. I can't say anything about the book except that I feel it is the story that I set out to tell."

In the same *School Library Journal* conversation, Collins explored the inherent humor in the *Scholastic* embargo. "I was saying to my husband, 'What am I going to say?' They won't even let him read the book. I don't have all this stuff that I can report about yet. Cap said 'Just tell them it's blue.' So I said 'Okay it's blue.'"

According to reports by *The Hollywood Reporter* and *Publishers Weekly*, *The Hunger Games* was published to what was described as 'modest' sales. But the trajectory changed when two heavy hitters in the literary community, Stephen King and *Twilight* author Stephenie Meyer, critically praised the book.

King, in his review of *The Hunger Games* for *Entertainment Weekly* compared the book to a multiplex video game. "You know it's not real but you keep plugging in quarters anyway."

The *New York Times* offered that the book was "brilliantly plotted and perfectly paced." *Time Magazine* praised the book by saying "It is a chilling, bloody and thoroughly horrifying book." *School Library Journal* called *The Hunger Games* "exciting, poignant, thoughtful and breathtaking by turns."

Suddenly *The Hunger Games* took off like a rocket.

CHAPTER TEN
The Fame Game

The response to Collins' *The Underlander Chronicles* fit the author to a T.

The reviews were positive. The sales were excellent. The consensus among literary observers was that Suzanne Collins was definitely making the leap from children's television writer to something special in the young adult literary world. But at the end of the day, the most important thing about the response was that she could still walk down the streets of her town and be… well just plain Suzanne to those around her.

But with the onset of *The Hunger Games*, those days were gone forever. Collins had morphed into everybody's next one, a media darling. For better or worse, she was no longer just plain Suzanne. She was now officially author celebrity de jour. The media shy, low key author would talk about how the change came about in *Deseret News*.

"I started to get phone calls from people I didn't know at my home number which, at the time, was not listed and we had never thought anything about it. Suddenly there was this shift. Nothing threatening happened or anything but it is your home and you want it to be private. So, I think that was the point where I felt 'Oh. Something different is happening here.'"

That something was an increase in media requests for interviews.

At that point, *Scholastic*, at Collins' request, put up a veil of limits around their prize author. Anything necessary to keep the public excited was filtered through a series of readily available and overtly softball and positive canned interviews conducted by the publisher in the comfort of their offices where Collins had grown to feel the most comfortable. Public appearances were limited and only important press had hopes of getting a one- on- one interview with the author.

And then there was the ultimate barometer of celebrity importance. The autograph.

To what degree Collins was amenable to signing books or just about anything else early on is not certain. But what is known among collectors was that by the time *The Hunger Games* kicked in, the author was increasingly reluctant to appear anywhere where her signature might be requested. Which made an actual signature, according to collectors' chat rooms and websites, worth anywhere from several hundred to several thousand dollars.

Around the time of the third book in *The Hunger Game* series, and on the occasion of a book store appearance in Michigan, the story was floated that Collins had developed Carpal Tunnell Syndrome and, according to reports from the scene, instead of an actual signature, the author had taken to stamping books with a stamp of her actual signature.

The David Bowie song 'Fame' would have the last word on the issue. Fame what's your name.

CHAPTER ELEVEN
Which Came First?

The novel *Battle Royal* would be written in 1996 but it would be three years later amid underground status in the literary community for its extreme violence and its fictional attacks on the then reigning Japanese government.

Battle Royale would tell the wildly dystopian tale of junior high school students forced to fight each other to the death in a program run by the shadowy fictional *Republic of Greater East Asia*. The book would spawn a movie and several magna stories and no small amount of controversy and notoriety.

Flash forward to (2008) and the publication of *The Hunger Games*. When a controversy of a different kind was brewing. Well-read readers of the dystopian/survivalist genre were quick to point out the plot similarities between *The Hunger Games* and *Battle Royale* and acknowledged that Collins would have had plenty of time to discover *Battle Royale* and incorporate certain of its elements into her book. It was not long before theory turned tabloid as the more cynical in the audience openly accused Collins of appropriating elements of *Battle Royale* into her own work. Soon the mainstream press were on the case with Collins responding to the *New York Times* on the matter.

"I have never heard of that book until I had turned

in the manuscript for *The Hunger Games*. At that point it was mentioned to me by an editor and I was asked if I had ever read it. I asked him if I should read it. He said no I don't want that world in your head. Just continue to do what you're doing."

A *New York Times* editorial assessment of the controversy indicated that there were enough possible sources that both the authors of *The Hunger Games* and *Battle Royale* could have independently come up with basically the same plot independently.

Historically speaking, literature exhibiting *Hunger Games* style literary tropes are a bit sketchy and just as plentiful.

But both *The New York Times* and the book *The Most Dangerous Cinema: People Hunting People* point to the 1924 short story *The Most Dangerous Game,* which appeared in *Colliers Magazine* on January 19, 1924 and which tells the story of a shipwrecked big game hunter being stalked by a Russian aristocrat on a deserted island, lays out a primitive blueprint of violence and psychological isolation. Two classics of literature *The Lottery* (Shirley Jackson) and *Lord of the Flies* (William Golding) effectively lay out, in subtle and raw moments the power and societal consequences of absolute control of one group over the other while the 1965 cult film *The 10th Victim*, based on the Robert Sheckley short story *Seventh Victim* ratchet up the suspense in a futuristic society where ratings are everything and the world quite literally can get away with murder for profit.

Of more recent vintage, the Stephen King novel *The Running Man* explores an interesting, very *Hunger Games* notion of violence as entertainment and television collide. Ever the controversial gadabout when not scaring the hell out of us, King, in conversation took some shots at *The Hunger Games* in conversation with *The Guardian*.

"I read *The Hunger Games* and did not feel any urge to go on. It's not unlike my book *The Running Man* which is about a game where people are actually killed and people are watching. It's a satire on reality television. And it's very derivative."

And at the end of the day, if you follow King's theory, and the success of *The Hunger Games* seems to prove that, if done the right way, derivative is not so bad.

CHAPTER TWELVE
Write the Sequel Yesterday

The final pages of *The Hunger Games'* manuscript were barely out of Collins' computer on their way to *Scholastic*. But the publisher's marketing people were already up and cooking on all cylinders.

Press releases and praise from important literary critics were flooding the blogosphere with raves heralding *The Hunger Games* as the next big wave of young adult literature and Collins as the next hot author on the heels of such queens of the genre as J.K. Rowling and Stephenie Meyer..

All Collins knew was that nobody had seen the book yet and *Scholastic* was already wanting to know if she could have the sequel to them in time for a 2009 release. Collins took the news in stride and just set about doing what all writers do... Which is to write.

"I felt like I had never left it (*The Hunger Games*), she related in a *Media Room.com Scholastic* interview. " The revisions on Book 1 overlapped with the writing of Book Two. Since each book feeds into the next, I feel like a part of my brain has been in *Panem* continuously."

Consequently, it came as no surprise when *Catching Fire* literally picked up where the last page of *The Hunger Games* ended. *Catching Fire* begins with Katniss glorying in the aftermath of her victory in *The Hunger Games*. Along the way she has angered *The Capitol* and threatened the status quo in *Panem* which has disrupted the political and social status of society. Katniss's celebrity driven victory lap is interrupted and she is drawn back into the game as the specter of a desperate government tries to hold back the shadow of rebellion and revolution that is suddenly upon it.

The consensus from a critical point of view was that *Catching Fire* is that Katniss was now more grownup and street smart. And those more observant readers were quick to spot that there was suddenly a deeper sense of Orwellian in the second chapter's storyline.

For her part, Collins saw the deeper probing of Katniss's psyche and character in *Catching Fire* as an indirect result of the countless war stories she heard from her military father while growing up. As she recalled in *Time Magazine*, her fighting heroine, whose actions are very much on display in the second half of *Catching Fire*, were typical of someone who had gone to war and had suffered the consequences.

"Katniss has a lot of classic post- traumatic stress disorder symptoms. She has nightmares. She has flashbacks. She's practicing avoidance with the likes of Peeta and Prim when she goes on her victory tour. In *Catching Fire*, she is a nightmare ready to happen."

By the time Collins sat down to write *Catching Fire*, her creative ducks were all very much in a row, with everything from her *NYU* dramatic writing influences to her children's television scriptwriting all very much in evidence when she sat down to sketch out the basic elements of the book as she explained in *Scholastic Media Room.com*. "I've learned that it helps me to work out the key structural points before I begin a story. The inciting incident, act breaks, mid story reversal, crisis and climax. I know a lot of what fills the spaces between those elements. But I also leave room for the characters to develop.

"If a door opens along the way and I'm intrigued by where it leads, I'll definitely go through it."

Critics were seemingly lining up to praise *Catching Fire*. *Booklit.com* opined "The unadorned prose provides an open window to perfect pacing and electrifying world building." *The New York Times* gushed "Collins has done that rare thing. She has written a sequel that improves upon that first book." *The Plain Dealer* cut to the critical chase when it said "The very last sentence in *Catching Fire* will leave readers gasping."

Collins would concede that at one point in her *Hunger Games* journey, that it was getting harder to indulge in her favorite pastimes, watching old black and white movies and getting a good night's sleep. And as she would acknowledge in *Book Page.com*, success was only breeding marginal leisure time with the family and the tube.

"It's been harder to write, especially last fall when I was promoting *The Hunger Games*, finishing *Catching Fire* and developing book three. The good news is, at this point, I think we're right on schedule."

CHAPTER THIRTEEN
Agree to Disagree

Collins is a born planner. So, the prospects for a book three in *The Hunger Games* odyssey? Quite simply, yes there would be a book three.

"I knew from the beginning there was going to be a trilogy," Collins matter of factly told *Book Page.com*.. "Once I thought through the events of the first book, I knew there would be repercussions from the events that would take place. So, I actually proposed it as a trilogy from the outset with the main story already laid out."

To say that the arrival of *Mockingjay* was an event of massive consequence in the publishing world and, in particular, in the halls of Scholastic was an understatement. After all, barring any future creative or financial considerations, this tale of the districts uniting to take on *The Capito*l were potentially massive in scope, with those actively speculating how it all would end.

By 2009, a file containing Collins' final manuscript of *Mockingjay* was winging its way through cyber space and into the computer of agent Rosemary Stimola who immediately opened the file and began to read.

As chronicled in the *New York Times*, her excitement was palpable. As she began to read, she was just as much fan as agent. But as she read, the agent in her began to emerge. Nearing the last few chapters, she came to the moment when a massive fire bomb kills thousands of civilians caught in the middle of the war. Stimola was stopped cold by the degree of violence that, even by Collins' standards, had been inserted into the final moments of *Mockingjay* and, by association, the conclusion of *The Hunger Games* saga.

The agent realized that the publication date for *Mockingjay* was quickly approaching and, as she dialed up Collins' phone number, she was thinking in terms of changes that could be made.

Stimola, paraphrasing what came next in the *New York Times* article, was quick and to the point when Collins picked up on the other end. "No!. Don't do it!" Collins would be quick on the defense of what would be too extreme even for young adult readers who had long since gotten used to the mature nature and messaging of *The Hunger Games* books. "Oh but it has to be," she countered. This is not a fairy tale. It's a war and in war there are tragic losses that must be mourned."

Of course, by the time Collins and Stimola were agreeing to disagree, the author had become fairly adept at defending her concept of reality in books meant largely for the young adult/teen market. Spirited defenses had become old hat as witness this excerpt from a less recent *New York Times* conversation.

"If we wait too long, what kind of expectations can we have (in introducing children to the reality of violence and war). We think we're sheltering them but what we're doing is putting them at a disadvantage."

Stimola hung up. Collins had won the war about war. *Mockingjay* would come out on time with the reality of this kind of life intact. Now it was up to the critics and, perhaps most importantly, the readers to tell the tale. Readers were primed to gobble *Mockingjay* up.

Publisher's Weekly called *Mockingjay* "A beautifully orchestrated and intelligent novel that succeeds on every level." *Entertainment Weekly* stated "Collins has kicked the brutal violence up a notch in an edge of your seat plot." And the *Los Angeles Times* ended its highly favorable review with a single word. "Wow!"

And in this clip of dialogue from *Mockingjay* by the character Katniss, there is a non too veiled warning of things to come.

"There are much worse games to play."

CHAPTER FOURTEEN
Lights, Camera, The Back Story

Suzanne Collins knew the value of her labor.

In pure materialistic terms, the success of *The Underland Chronicles* and *The Hunger Games* series of books had put the notoriously frugal author on easy street. But Collins was aware that the financial floodgates as well as challenges to her creative ethics were about to open and to be tested.

Collins had barely completed her final writing and editing on *Mockingjay* in March 2009. But the perceived occasion of *The Hunger Games* officially coming to an end in book form (it would still be another year before *Mockingjay* was officially published) would be pretty much over shadowed by the fact that Hollywood was now officially free, according to the fine print on the author's early *Hunger Games'* contract, to make the books into movies, starting with *The Hunger Games*.

As chronicled in the likes of *The Hollywood Reporter*, *Reuters*, *Publishers Weekly* and a whole lot of other outlets, the production company *The Color Force* had swooped in early in March and acquired worldwide distribution rights to the novel. Collins agent Jason Davis, in a *Reuters* interview, acknowledged that the production company *The Color Force*, and in particular its head Nina Jacobson, had the inside track on the rights issue. "Jacobson had worked on big franchises before. We knew this novel [*The Hunger Games*] had the potential to get very dark very quickly and she (Jacobson) understood how to keep it from doing that."

Two weeks after *The Color Force* deal closed, *Lionsgate Films* was pulling out every conceivable stop to land *The Hunger Games* film rights according to *Reuters* and the *Box Office History of Lionsgate Movies.com*.

Lionsgate, still considered an upstart in the movie business which reportedly, had not made a profit in five years, cobbled together a money bid for *The Hunger Games'* film rights by raiding the budgets of some of their other productions and selling off company assets in order to bring an $88 million dollar offer to the table.

But beyond financial considerations, Lionsgate's insistence that they would stay true to the novel ultimately won Collins over according to her agent Jason Davis in *Reuters*. "When the Lionsgate head of marketing told us he had mapped out exactly how *Lionsgate* would market the film she [Collins] felt it would be in good hands."

While she was confident that Lionsgate knew what they were doing, Collins acknowledged that she was new to the idea of filmmaking, especially when it came to the all-important element of casting and, in particular, the role of the heroine that was the lynchpin of *The Hunger Games*. Her creative insecurities were very much in evidence in *Entertainment Weekly*.

"As the author, I went into the casting process with a certain degree of trepidation. Believing your heroine can make the leap from the relative safety of the page to the flesh and bones reality of the screen is something of a creative leap of faith. But after watching dozens of auditions by a group of fine young actresses, I felt there was only one who truly captured the character I wrote in the book and I am thrilled to say that Jennifer Lawrence has accepted the role. I think the essential question for me was would she believably inspire a rebellion? Did she project the strength, defiance and intellect you would need to follow her into war? For me she did."

That emotional and mental issue resolved, Collins would remain adamant in having her hand in the creative side of things and would ultimately come away with a percentage of the film's profits, active participation in the screen writing process and onscreen credit. There was also talk of the author coming away with some kind of producers' title on any and all *Hunger Games* films.

It went without saying that Collins came away from the deal quite wealthy. But, most importantly, with a firm contract grip on how *The Hunger Games* was to be handled by Hollywood.

Now it was time to get to work.

But, as she would offer in *Entertainment Weekly*, she was cautious about the opportunity. "In the beginning, when I attached myself as the screenwriter, I was still writing the third book and there was great secrecy about it. At that point, no one could know how it ended. But I knew that if the screenplay got off on the wrong foot, you could end up with something by which you could never reach the events of the third book to the film team.

"I wanted to be around to keep an eye on that."

CHAPTER FIFTEEN
An Enormously Tricky Thing To Do

From the moment Collins conceived the idea of *The Hunger Games*, she knew, on a level fairly high in her psyche, that someday there would be a movie. She also knew two things.

She would be involved in the screenplay and, despite having a background in drama and television story-telling, for the author it would be an enormously tricky thing to do. When it was time to make *The Hunger Games* into a cinema reality, she told the New York Times that while she was up to the task, it would not be a walk in the park.

"I did the boil down of the book which was a lot of cutting things while trying to retain the dramatic structure. I think the hardest thing for me, because I'm not a terribly visual person, was finding the way to translate many words into a few images."

The psychological intimacy Collins had with her creation was obvious and she acknowledged the level of challenge involved in translating *The Hunger Games* from page to screen in a conversation with *Entertainment Weekly*. "Obviously you have to let things go. But it's more than a question of condensation. You want to preserve the essence while making the film stand on its own. It's an art in itself."

But this being Hollywood, Collins would soon find that she had a lot of help and that creative moments were more often a by-product of a committee. In this case, Collins wrote the initial treatments and the first draft of the script. Subsequent drafts were written in conjunction with screen writer/director Gary Ross and screenwriter Billy Ray.

In an *Entertainment Weekly* article, Collins reported that the collaboration was all good. "Lionsgate established a dialogue with me, they made me feel that my input was valuable and welcome."

Given the egos rampant in Hollywood, it would almost be beyond belief that all the creative elements attached to *The Hunger Games* script would have such good chemistry from the get go. But if screenwriter and soon-to-be director of *The Hunger Games* is to be believed in conversation with *WGA.com*, the relationship between Collins and himself was just too good to be true.

"I wrote a draft of my own which was very faithful to the book. Suzanne liked it a lot, gave me some notes and came out to visit me in California. We started talking to each other even though we weren't working together yet and that conversation was so electric and spontaneous that within an hour we were working together."

In a *Hollywood Reporter* interview, Ross was pretty much at a loss as to the tenor of the conversations he had with Collins during the writing phase of *The Hunger Games* script. "There were so many conversations with Suzanne that it is hard to narrow them down to a single thing. One thing I did find fascinating was how stepped she was in Roman history. In *The Hunger Games* she was exploring how a culture devolves into spectacle and Rome was her starting point."

Suzanne Collins, The Hunger GamesMaker

Script completed, *The Hunger Games* went before the cameras in North Carolina . Collins would make herself present during some of the casting sessions and, reportedly, good naturedly turned down the opportunity to do an acting bit in the film. But, in a very real sense, the beginning of filming on *The Hunger Games* signaled a new phase in her creative life and with some time off to catch her breath, she contemplated the transition from book to cinema and, not surprisingly, was introspective in assessing the two media she now encompassed.

"Because the film is a faithful adaptation of the story, that becomes the primary thing. Some people will never read a book but they might see the same story in a movie. When it works well, the two entities support and enrich each other."

CHAPTER SIXTEEN
Welcome to the Jungle

Two thousand twelve would be a banner year for Suzanne Collins.

Submitted in evidence the following. On March 2012, Collins was named the best-selling kindle author of all time by Amazon. The Hunger Games film was an international box office smash on arrival, collecting $695.2 million in ticket sales. And finally, the ink had barely dried on the previous tally when Lionsgate announced with all public relations guns blazing that *The Hunger Games: Catching Fire* film, which was nowhere near casting and production, would be released in November 2013.

One bit of note that had almost gone completely unnoticed during this period was a bit of moonlighting from being a best-selling author was a script writing chore in a direct-to-video thriller called *Ticket Out* (2012) which told the nail-biting tale of an unhappy woman fleeing the clutches of her crazed husband. This film disappeared without a trace but is available if you look hard enough.

One bit of news that almost escaped acknowledgment around that time, as reported by *The Wrap.com* by Collins' agent Jason Davis who said matter of fact that Collins had no plans to write a fourth *Hunger Games* book. "Another one? No. The books are done." Whether that bit of news would actually turn out to be true remained to be seen.

In the meantime, Collins was in a state of bliss. Secure in the knowledge that, with the completion of *The Hunger Games: Mockingjay*, *The Hunger Games* saga was, at the very least, on hold as any future adventures in that universe was concerned. But her creative instincts were quick to acknowledge that there would be something else in the offing. And as it would turn out, what would follow would be the most personal, and yes very autobiographical, story she had ever written.

It was a look at the ramifications of war told from the point of view of the very young called *Year of the Jungle*. Collins had often referenced her real-life memories of her father's military service as a major influence in her writing. But with *Year of the Jungle*, Collins would meet his influence on her life head on in a most personal way.

Year of the Jungle was an idea that Collins had been contemplating since 2010 and, as she acknowledged in *The Christian Science Monitor*, it was the completion of a goal that would allow the concept and meaning of war to be explored in all age groups. "My goal was to write a book about war that very young children could understand."

The very autobiographical tale takes place in the 60's when a young first grader named Suzy is struggling to understand why her military father has been sent off to a place called Vietnam. She understands little at first, imaging Vietnam as a jungle where she would romp and play with animals. This child-like vision is suddenly shattered when while watching the news, she discovers the real frights of a place where her father has been sent. Initially she would be comforted by the letters and postcards her father would send her but suddenly the letters and postcards stopped coming. Suzy is anxious

Suzanne Collins, The Hunger GamesMaker

that her father may have changed while he was in Vietnam. Eventually Suzy's father does return and Suzy notices the difference in him. He has changed and she wonders how those changes will affect their relationship.

It went without saying that Collins was channeling some deep, personal and very real emotions in this story that would be daring in its deliberate telling of a four-year-old and up readership. Obviously, Collins had described her childhood and her military father on several occasions in the past. But in describing *Year of the Jungle* with *Time*, there was a renewed sense of how her real life was now translating into real art.

"If I took the 40 years of my dad talking to me about war and battles and distilled it all down to one question, it would probably be the idea of the necessary and unnecessary war. This book is really just an introduction to the idea of war for very young children."

In reflecting on the origin of *Year of the Jungle* in the Associated Press and CBS News, the author did bring up an element of her own childhood memories of a dad at war as well as what she perceived as the biggest challenge in writing what was, on the surface, a very simplistic picture book that would top out at 40 pages of story and illustration.

"For several years I had this little wicker basket next to my writing chair with the postcards and notes my father had sent me from that year in Vietnam. But I could never quite find a way into the story because it has elements that can be scary for a four-year-old audience. It would be easy for the art to reinforce those scares. It could be beautiful art but still be off putting to a kid which would defeat the point of doing the book."

That's when she reconnected with her mentor from

the children's television days, James Proimos. Proimos had remained a largely under the radar presence when it came to illustrating books and by 2013, and as documented in a PR Newswire story, stated that "I had decided not to draw a single thing for a year and would only concentrate on my writing."

Proimos's decision was short-lived as he recalled in PR Newswire during one of their occasional get togethers for lunch. "In fact I told this to Suzanne only minutes before she asked me to illustrate her next book."

Collins recalled that moment in conversation with the Associated Press. "I was having lunch with Jim and telling him about the idea I had and he said 'that sounds fantastic.' I looked at him and had this flash of the story through his eyes and his art. It was like being handed a key to a locked door. I blurted out 'do you want to do it?' Fortunately he said yes."

Proimos, told the Associated Press, that he instinctively saw the merits of *Year of the Jungle*. "How could I refuse? The idea that she laid out was brilliant. It was not like any picture book I had ever come across. The writing was moving and personal. What Suzanne does so well with this book is convey the complicated emotions through the eyes of a child."

Year of the Jungle was published in late August 203. The difference between the roll out of this book, despite it being Suzanne Collins' first post Hunger Games book was apparent. The hype was well mannered rather than frantic, more respectful and, by degrees, more thoughtful. None of which prevented *Year of the Jungle* from being a success, albeit a low key one, that was much appreciated and critically acclaimed. Readers most certainly got it. Just not in the same way.

Collins would sense that *Year of the Jungle* would have a different kind of success and hoped against hope that it would not be a book that, after a few reads, would be put away on a shelf.

In Suzanne Collins.com, the author gave her wish list for the book. "I hope that people will read the book even if they don't have a deployed family member. Even if they are not part of a military family, maybe it will help other kids understand what other kids from military families are going through. "

CHAPTER SEVENTEEN
Hollywood Catches Fire

There was no question about it. *The Hunger Games: Catching Fire* was going to be made.

You don't just arbitrarily say thanks but no thanks to a phenomenon that has become so big so fast. If the theater owners and, lest we forget, the people at Lionsgate and Suzanne Collins herself, stand to make millions by the time the dust settles on the first take on the set of *Catching Fire*, the question was not so much if but when the sequel would be made.

But in typical Hollywood fashion, getting to that first shot was not completely smooth sailing according to the outlets *The Wrap.com*, *The Hollywood Reporter* and *Entertainment Weekly*.

Screenwriter Simon Beaufoy would write two drafts of the *Catching Fire* script before leaving along with director Gary Ross who had, in turn left the project when objecting to the task of writing and directing the sequel in the compressed time of three months after the release of the first film to accommodate star Jennifer Lawrence's obligation to the latest *X Men* movie. Ross would ultimately be replaced by director Francis Lawrence.

For her part, Collins would watch the way the situation was being handled in a state of bliss. According to credit watchers, Collins would receive a nominal nod as screenwriter/story in *Catching Fire* as well as the title of Executive Producer, what many would consider a nominal award for services rendered on the creative front.

Although she would be contacted on occasion to comment on certain elements of the book's translation to the screen, she was largely free of any obligation outside of a few selected interviews, which would include praise for Lionsgate's handling of the sequel and to reflect on the sequel and where she was at with what *The Hunger Games* books and now movies had brought her.

As she offered in a *Time Magazine* interview, it's all free and easy on the occasions when she did visit the *Catching Fire* set and witnessed what had quickly evolved by the start of the second film into a well-oiled movie making machine.

"I visit on set. But I feel like there's really nothing for me to do in terms of work. It's like you go to the set and everybody has a job but you. I feel very comfortable about whatever is transpiring on the set whether I'm there or not which is nice."

And on the occasion when she did encounter the press during the making of *Catching Fire*, she found a media that did not stray too far from lobbing the by now familiar softball questions for Collins to hit. One of the more playful being whether or not she would be inclined to do a cameo in *Catching Fire*. "I'm not tempted to be in the film at all," she told *Time Magazine*. "I'm not comfortable around cameras."

But as *Catching Fire* ground steadily to a finished film, Collins, in a more contemplative moment away from the world's perception of her as a pop culture/celebrity author maven, told *Time Magazine*, "I have read so many interpretations of the books and the story and the movies. But for me it's always been a war story. But, ultimately, whatever brings you to the story is fine with me. For me, it's a war story. But for me it also has so many ethical issues just because you're dealing with war. You can't both write and then sit up on the other side and interpret it for people.

"My attitude is come for the love story and stay for the war."

CHAPTER EIGHTEEN
The Ex... Or Are They?

Yes, Suzanne Collins does or did have a better half. And yes they did have two children. But beyond those basics, the relationship remains a bit on the murky side.

We know that Collins and Charles Cap Pryor met at Indiana University. We know they fell in love, had two children while living in New York and eventually moved to Sandy Hook, Connecticut and lived an idyllic, quiet life while Collins set about creating a worldwide phenomenon.

But here's some things about Collins' husband that may have slipped through the proverbial cracks.

While living in New York and while Collins was beginning her career writing for children's television, Pryor was scuffling with bit parts and production gigs in television, reality shows and low-budget movies. These included *One Among Us*, *Co Ed Confidential*, *Cable Con Leche*. *The Last POW? The Bob Garwood Story* and, coincidentally, an acting gig in an episode of the Collins' scripted television show *The Mystery Files of Shelby Woo*. Pryor also held down the occasional teaching job with an emphasis on special needs children.

By the time Collins and Pryor left New York for a quieter and much less crowded Connecticut, it most likely transpired quite naturally that Pryor would take over much of the house hold duties and much of the care and supervision of the couple's two children. For his part, Pryor seemed okay with his status as house husband and it had been reported on several occasions that he often edited early drafts of *The Hunger Games.*

Over the years Collins' interviews rarely touched on her relationship with her husband, which may well have been the result of the regimented nature of her dealings with the media. But in *Suzanne Collins Books.com*, the author did bring up Pryor and acknowledged him as a force in her creative life.

"My husband Cap would be great to have in *The Underland* since he is very good in an emergency. But I would want him to be with our kids in *The Overland*. Cap says he would not take me to *The Underland* because I am not good in an emergency and I would constantly make him stop and ask for directions."

On the surface, their relationship remained seemingly ideal. Pryor and Collins were regularly photographed at special events, all smiles and holding hands. These are the fragmentary realities of their relationship. What would follow in recent years are waves of questionable/tabloid style bits.

IMDB.com was one of the first outlets to claim that Collins and Pryor divorced in 2015. *Tick Tock.com* loudly speculated that Collins had asked Pryor for a divorce. *Book Analysis.com* offered up the notion that the couple had, in fact, been separated but not divorced since 2015. Countering the notion that whatever was going on in their personal lives remained amicable would be the 2020 novel *The Ballad of Songbirds and Snakes* in which Collins referred to Pryor as her husband on the acknowledgements page.

Suzanne Collins, The Hunger GamesMaker

Bottom line, whatever the status of their relationship is ultimately remains a mystery to fans and followers of the author and her life who want to know it all.

Because neither Collins nor Pryor are talking.

CHAPTER NINETEEN
Was Two Mockingjays Too Much?

Two important days to mark on your Hunger Games calendar. May 2012. Lionsgate announces the start of development on *The Hunger Games: Mockingjay*. On July 2012, Lionsgate announced that the film version of *Mockingjay* would be split into two separate films.

The bombshell did not go unnoticed.

And the at large perception was that *Mockingjay* the book, which clocked in at 390 pages would have made one ideal movie wrap up to the trilogy. But the notion was that while one, fairly long film version of *Mockingjay* might have presented a satisfactory conclusion to *The Hunger Games* saga, a literal translation might also make for a very long movie. And the announcement of a two -film *Mockingjay* split barely hit the media waves when the proposed two film split was met with both film critics and fans alike weighing in.

The deep concern was that the *Mockingjay* book, split in two could well fall victim to padding and long dull stretches where nothing much was going on. But the reality was that diehard fans would flock to the theaters to see *Mockingjay* no matter how many films they had to see. And at the end of the day, it would be money and Lionsgate's drive to milk Collins' story for all the money it could that ultimately drove the decision.

For her part, Collins had always been a good soldier when it came to Lionsgate's decisions. With her executive producer title still on the boards, she must have had some say in the matter. Her take on the matter was never truly explored however. But what is known, according to *Buzz Feed.com*, is that she would do her best to make a two film *Mockingjay* work.

Adding his own bit of controversy was director Francis Lawrence who was slated to direct both *Mockingjay* films when he stated that he was less than thrilled with the idea of directing two films in what he felt would have been a perfectly good single film based on Collins' book. "I totally regret it. I totally do. I'm not sure everybody else does but I definitely do."

But thinking better of the notion of biting the hand that was feeding him, Lawrence followed, in *People*, with a more measured explanation.

"I was able to get more from the book by breaking it up into two parts. The team agreed that the two films had their own separate questions that needed to be answered which allowed the filmmakers to tell two complete story arcs. In truth, we got more on the screen out of the book then we would have in the two previous books because we were getting close to four hours of screen time from *Mockingjay*."

But in the end it would all boil down to getting a lot of butts in the seats which thanks to a multi-pronged event style marketing campaign that was ultimately designed to do just that.

Despite the two *Mockingjay* films being released a year apart, a box office smash was almost assured. The audience for *The Hunger Games* was too wide and universal and was set in stone. All the controversy and speculation in the world was not going to keep the final two films in *The Hunger Games* saga from being a success of immense proportions.

The movies made untold millions which made Lionsgate happy. The filmmakers were over the moon with their creative efforts. And most likely the happiest of all was Collins. A big part of her creative life had been directed into the three books and the subsequent movies and to know that her books were now set in classic proportions and a part of literary and cinematic history was beyond just rewards for a job well done.

With the conclusion of the final *Hunger Games* films, Collins put out a heartfelt message of thanks to the filmmakers and fans who made her *Hunger Games* life so rewarding.

"Thank you for volunteering for *The Games* and inhabiting these characters with such texture, color, humor and pain," she reflected in an excerpt of her letter. "Having spent the last decade in Panem, it's time to move on to other lands. But before I do I'd like to say a tremendous thank you to everyone associated with the film franchise. I'm thrilled with how this quartet of films, which I have found both faithful to the books and innovative in their own right, has been brought to life on the screen. To all the readers and the viewers who have accompanied Katniss on her journey, thank you for playing a role in The Hunger Games.

"You are truly a vital part of the experience."

CHAPTER TWENTY
Okay What's Next?

It's time to move onto other lands. The words hung in the fanbase of *The Hunger Games* like an anticipatory cloud. Pure and simple, what is next for Suzanne Collins?

Between 2014 and 2019, Suzanne Collins, creatively and otherwise, was not to be found.

Media observers and fans were quick to quite simply point out that the author was taking a well- deserved vacation, enjoying being with her family, spending some of her massive amounts of *Hunger Games* money and being other than the celebrity author who created a worldwide sensation. It would not be the first time a superstar author has ducked out.

J.K. Rowling, after years of being the "it" author of *Harry Potter*, has to a large extent, been largely missing in action and has been, for the most part, hard to find ever since. The same goes for Stephenie Meyer who, since the mania for *Twilight* has subsided, has also been far from the pop culture sights.

But Collins' disappearing act has been fairly recent and so there has been the inevitable waves of 'what's next?' Colliins' agent, Jason Davis has continued his mantra of "the books are done." And such websites as *The Wrap*, *Screen Rant* and *Dexerto* have taken turns dissecting the minute' of how and why there will or will not be another *Hunger Games* book.

Ironically it would be the person most inclined to support more *Hunger Games*, film producer Nina Jacobson, who, in *Yahoo Entertainment.com* and *Polygon.com* would make the most realistic defense of not rushing Collins in any way, shape or form.

"If Suzanne has something to say, then she will write a book about it. Honestly, as much as I love Katniss, I think her story is complete. But if that changes and Suzanne has something she wants to say and it involves Katniss, then I would be thrilled."

In the same moments, Jacobson deftly deflected the rumors that Lionsgate was thinking about filling in the gaps of Collins' absence with spinoffs or reboots of *The Hunger Games*. "Collins would have to write the novel for one thing. If Collins had a story to tell in this world, with something she wanted to talk about, something to explore, then great. But, if not, better to leave a franchise as something people feel fondly about rather than crank out a sequel for the sake of a sequel.

Long story short. When Collins has something to say, the world will jump for joy. But not before.

And this is where things get murky.

CHAPTER TWENTY-ONE
Who Owns The Hunger?

On June 17, 2019, it was announced that the prequel to *The Hunger Games* series, *The Ballad of Songbirds and Snakes*, was to be published on May 19, 2020. The hype on that front had barely settled when Lionsgate, on August 17, 2020, announced that they would be making a movie out of the book. No surprise there.

It was almost after the fact that Collins had been writing *The Ballad of Songbirds and Snakes* since 2016. Amid the expected hoopla from fandom, a much darker aspect of everybody's favorite dystopian teen adventures began to emerge.

Who was driving *The Hunger Games* express? Suzanne Collins or Hollywood?

If one were to read the fine print it would become evident that... Collins owns the rights to *The Hunger Games* books. But, wading through the Hollywood fun and games, it was Collins who, in fact, signed over the film rights to *The Hunger Games*, albeit for a king's ransom in cash and film credits.

Around the time that Scholastic was announcing the impending release of *The Ballad of Songbirds and Snakes*, there were signs that the Hollywood side of *The Hunger Games* phenomena might well be hedging its bets.

As early as 2013, Lionsgate was already stretching the marketing possibilities of *The Hunger Games* franchise when it made a deal for a *Hunger Games* theme park with the country of United Arab Emirates in Dubai. By 2016, the company closed a deal for a theatrical stage presentation of *The Hunger Games* to be staged in London. There was also some fairly serious talk along the halls of Lionsgate of a *Hunger Games* television series.

Perhaps thinking that they might be sending the wrong message with exploiting so many ancillary markets, Lionsgate CEO Jon Feltheimer, at a quarterly earnings report covered by the likes of *Variety* and *The Hollywood Reporter* struck a more diplomatic rather than mercenary tone when he offered "We are always looking for ways to extend all of our intellectual properties."

In the same meeting, Feltheimer further offered, "The company will only go forward with fresh installments or spinoffs (including a long-speculated *Hunger Games* television series) if they get the sign off from Suzanne Collins. There are a lot more stories to be told and we are ready to tell them when our creators are ready to tell those stories."

This offering of a diplomatic smokescreen might well be the mantra going forward, perhaps to placate the fans who were not, to a large extent, upset about the ancillary spin offs and, perhaps most importantly, to not ruffle the feathers of Collins. Film producer Nina Jacobson, in several media outlets including *Comic Book* Resources echoed the fact that "Lionsgate isn't planning to make any more films unless Collins writes more books to adapt."

Anyone hoping for a more definitive comment from Collins herself may well have been in for a long wait. On the rare occasion when the author had issued a statement, she had continued to be a politically correct good soldier.

"Lionsgate has been a wonderful home and partner for *The Hunger Games* franchise."

Producer Jacobson would make a spirited final defense of *The Hunger Games* continuing in one form or another in *Comic Book Resources*. "It would be unwise to make more *Hunger Games* movies without the proper source material. But I believe that audiences can still learn a lot from the franchise."

CHAPTER TWENTY-TWO
When In Doubt… Songbirds and Snakes

We knew it was coming.

Even the most patient *Hunger Games* fans were starting to get a shade antsy. Yes the author had been working on the first *Hunger Games* follow up for quite some time now. Not unexpectedly, it was time for the hype machine, canned Suzanne Collins interview leading the march, to leave the station. The best seller status had been assured months ago. Collins had signed on the proverbial dotted line for the by now inevitable film adaptation.

But after a ten-year book hiatus, marked by film adaptations going on forever, was *The Ballad of Songbirds and Snakes* really what the world expected? Or wanted? The consensus in the *Hunger Games* fan universe was that the last book in the initial storyline should be the end. Sequels were talked about and Collins continued to fan the flames by offering that another *Hunger Games* storyline might just appear under the right circumstances.

As it turned out *The Ballad of Songbirds and Snakes* was set not only to take the odyssey forward but, perhaps most importantly, back to where much of the original storyline began. As prequels go, *The Ballad of Songbirds and Snakes* is pretty sturdy stuff. Taking *The Hunger Games* conceit back to the time of the *10th Hunger Game* and centering on the life of future president Coriolanus Snow, some 64 years before the events of *The Hunger Games*.

Producer Nina Jacobson offered in a *Variety* conversation that the storyline of *Ballad of Songbirds and Snakes* appeared to be a courageous creative step on the part of Collins. "But I loved what Suzanne did. If you had asked fans what they wanted in the next story, I don't think anybody would have said 'I want the villain origin story.' You want to see the people you like, not the person we've worked so hard to hate."

Many in the shortsighted critical community saw the storyline as a good commercial move designed to prolong and expand the brand for years to come. But Collins, in an interview that was excerpted by such outlets as *The Hollywood Reporter* and *Deadline.com*, was earnest in defining *The Ballad of Songbirds and Snakes* as something much deeper.

"In this book I use the world of *Panem* to explore the elements of the just war theory. Focusing on the *10th Hunger Game* gave me the opportunity to tell the Lucy Gray story that is mentioned in the first chapter of the very first *Hunger Games* book. I really enjoyed going back in time to an earlier version of *The Hunger Games*, the reconstruction period that followed *The Dark Days*. With this book I wanted to explore the state of nature, who we are and what we perceive is required for our survival. The *10th Hunger Games* is pivotal to the *Hunger Games* story because this is where it all blows open."

The Ballad of Songbirds and Snakes was published with the expected hype and hoopla and was an immediate best seller much in the tradition of the previous *Hunger Games* books. There would be the odd critical observations about the length of the book, a shade over 500 pages, and the notion that some elements of the book, whether intentional or not, bordered on parody. But for the most part, critics seemed to have figured Collins' method to *The Hunger Games* and said as much.

The Guardian praised the book when it offered "Collins' themes of friendship, betrayal, authority and oppression will please and thrill." *Time Magazine* pointed out that "She weaves in fantasizing details that lend depth to the gruesome world she created in the original series." *Kirkus Reviews* called the book "a tense, character driven piece and a cautionary tale."

The critics could not be trifled with. At the end of the day, *The Ballad of Songbirds and Snakes* proved that Collins had the Midas Touch and that she could do no wrong.

CHAPTER TWENTY-THREE
Songbirds and Snakes: The Movie

And then came *Hunger Games: The Ballad of Songbirds and Snakes: The Movie.*

The announcement that there would be a movie came as a surprise to absolutely nobody and Collins was thrilled at the prospect that it came together like a well-oiled machine as reported by such diverse outlets as *Den of Geeks.com* and *Deadline.com*.

Francis Lawrence, who had directed the previous three *Hunger Games* films was back to direct. Script writers Michael Arndt and Michael Lesslie, with credited assistance from Collins who would also be rewarded with another production credit, knocked out a satisfactory version of the book in record time.

The only real concern was how the lengthy book would translate as a movie, which was already being speculated to be a three hour film. For a time, there was fairly serious talk, primarily from Lionsgate, about turning *The Ballad of Songbirds and Snakes* into two separate films ala what transpired with *The Hunger Games: Mockingjay.* It was a notion that was almost immediately dismissed by just about everybody connected with the film, most notably director Francis Lawrence who said as much in a conversations with *Entertainment Weekly* and *People*.

"The film was shaping up to be nearly three hours long and there was like one second that I thought 'Do we want two movies?' What I realized in retrospect and after hearing the reactions of the fans, people and critics about the split of *Mockingjay* is that I realized it was frustrating and I decided that we were not going down that road again."

Filming began in Poland in July, 2022 and concluded in Germany in November 2022. Collins once again proved to be the de facto cheerleader for the film. She was quick to praise the cast and crew. Things were always right in her world and she was always on board to tell her fans as much.

Collins' confidence would be rewarded on May 19, 2022 when *The Ballad of Songbirds and Snakes* was released internationally. When the dust settled the film's initial theatrical release had grossed $350 million.

CHAPTER TWENTY-FOUR
Hunger Raises the Curtain

If ever there was a Hollywood match made in heaven, the relationship between Suzanne Collins and Lionsgate would have to be right up there in terms of compatibility. Collins had been left alone to do her thing and Lionsgate had been conspicuous by their ability to leave her alone.

But the company has also been quite judicious in taking Collins world and moving it along to different media and possibilities. Such was the case in 2023 when the author was first presented with the notion of bringing the world of *The Hunger Games* to the stage.

Thus was born *Hunger Games: The Stage Experience*, a multimedia, immersive experience adapted from the first *Hunger Games* book and the subsequent film. The conceit was an ambitious one, a theatrical approach in an in the round experience.

The production was conceived with a very British sensibility in mind, directed by Matthew Dunster and award-winning playwright Connor McPherson and was slated for an October 25, 2025 run in the UK's Troubadour Canary Wharf Theater which was custom built to accommodate the in-the-round experience for an audience of 1200.

Originally discussed as a 2024 production, *Hunger Games: The Stage Experience* was pushed back a year so that the production could be effectively workshopped to fine tune what was shaping up as dizzying array of stunts, flying and choreography.

Needless to say, Collins was very much in the mix when it came to the development process and, as she stated in a prepared statement which was quickly snapped up by international media, she was quite happy with the results.

"It is a brand-new way to experience the story," she enthused. "I'm thrilled with the theatrical concept and the immersive dynamic staging will give the audience a new way to experience *The Hunger Games* story."

Tickets for the theatrical production officially went on sale on March 27, 2025 and became an instant sell out, assuring that *The Hunger Games: The Stage Experience* was due for a long run in the UK and, ultimately, a concept that would go on forever.

For her part, Collins was thrilled. But by that time, the author already had something else on her plate.

CHAPTER TWENTY-FIVE
The Reaping Keeps Hunger Alive

Going into 2024, there was much evidence that *The Hunger Games* odyssey still, creatively, had a ways to go.

The success of the prequel *The Ballad of Songbirds and Snakes* had exhibited the kind of critical and commercial success that both the fans and the Hollywood bean counters had hoped for. The notion that continuing *Hunger* books might rise and fall on Collins ability to keep the main characters from the first four books was laid to rest

And as had always been with the author, Collins sat down at the computer screen, she had another idea, her fingers hit the keyboard and the magic once again began to unfold.

Sunrise on the Reaping was about to be born. And, as explored by producer Nina Jacobson in *Variety,* it was a clandestine bit of business. "This was a very different process for us. We never actually worked on a film adaptation like this where we were so far ahead of the book being published. I knew Suzanne was working on another book but I really had no idea. It could be years away. I did not expect that so soon after *Ballad* that I would be getting a call from Suzanne saying 'I have another book and I want you to read it. I want to know whether you think it's a movie or not."

Jacobson recalled that what followed was right out of a spy thriller. "We had to do a whole secret thing. I went to her agent's house and read it. There was only one copy of the book and that lived at her agent's house. By the time I finished reading it, I was on the edge of my seat crying. I was so moved by it."

From the outset, Collins sensed that she had found a way to backtrack to the events that took place prior to the first *Hunger Games* adventure and to make it plausible in terms of what had come before and, at the same time, continue the sense of emotion and character that had highlighted the original stories.

Sunrise on the Reaping takes a leap forward from the events of *The Ballad of Songbirds and Snakes* by focusing on events that take place 24 years before the onset of the original *Hunger Games* and focuses on the morning of the *50th Hunger Game* in which the character Haymitch Abernathy must navigate a world which has become even more dystopian under the strident hand of Corolanus Snow who, since the previous book has grown into the villain readers are by now all too familiar with. This book is a fairly ruthless bit of business in which Haymitch uses his guile to capture the *50th Hunger Game* but, by book's end, ends up paying a stiff price for it.

If there was a challenge to be had in writing *Sunrise on the Reaping*, it boiled down to how to portray the titular character of Haymitch as Collins explored in *People*. "I considered keeping Haymitch an adult character for a while. I played around with it both ways but I found that the younger Haymitch speaks directly to the young adult audience the best. An older person reflecting back on their youth or shifting into a child's perspective is harder to pull off. I don't think it changed my understanding of him. Haymitch is still Haymitch."

Suzanne Collins, The Hunger GamesMaker

As the book made its way through the final editing process on its way to a March 18, 2025 publication date, bits and pieces of the storyline inevitably leaked out and the latest wave of media inquiry and speculation began with such media outlets as *AP News*, *ABC News*, *USA Today* and *Screen Rant* making their inquiring minds present in the author's world. As always, Collins was ready with the answers.

"I was inspired to write *Sunrise on the Reaping* by reading Scottish philosopher David Humes' idea of implicit submission and the easiness with which the many are governed by the few. The story also lent itself to a deeper dive into the use of propaganda and the power of those who control the narrative. The question of real or not real seems more pressing to me every day."

As the *Hunger Games* countdown to publishing *Sunrise on The Reaping* neared, Scholastic went all out in priming the hype machine. A week before the March 18 release of the book, the publishing company released an audio of Collins reading an excerpt of the forthcoming book. Book stores were also getting into the spirit and excitement of the event with *Hunger Games* themed store windows, midnight release parties and all manner of in-store promotions. The vibe surrounding the release of the new book was nothing if not joyous.

And critics were happy to pile on.

The New York Times trumpeted the book when it reported "It is with great pleasure that I can report that *Sunrise on The Reaping* is a propulsive, heart wrenching addition to the *Games*, adding welcome texture to the cruel world of *Panem*."

The Guardian praised the author. "Collins is an excellent writer and there are moments of surprising lyricism which help to leaven the grimness."

People raved positive. "It's a life-giving book. It reminds us that unity is worth something."

The bookstore festivities were well attended by members of the Scholastic publishing family. Noticeably absent from any and all appearances was Collins, not a surprise as the publicity-shy author had long proclaimed her shyness about such events. Scholastic marketing executive Rachel Coun, in conversation with *Variety*, made a strong defense of Collins being a no show at such events.

"At the end of the day, it's about the book. That's what it's all about. If you write a brilliant book, people are going to respond to it and it's going to be timeless."

In the middle of the celebration, Scholastic boss Ellie Berger was heaving a sigh of relief that *Sunrise on The Reaping* came as a surprise to readers as she related in *Variety*. "You always worry about leaks. It's been really scary on this book. There have been no big leaks to spoil things and that surprised me because it's been much harder to avoid leaks these days. Now with social media and how things can be posted online so quickly, it's just harder and the stakes are higher. Fortunately, with this book everything has turned out okay."

To the surprise of absolutely no one. Lionsgate jumped the gun on *Sunrise on the Reaping* announced on June 6, 2024 when it said that the film version of a book that was not yet completed was going into immediate pre-production and slated to be in theaters on November 20, 2026. But when *Sunrise on the Reaping* was published on March 18, 2025 and the inevitable mania and best seller levels ensued, Lionsgate could be forgiven cocksure pronouncements.

Because *Sunrise on the Reaping* had once again proven that there was such a thing as a sure thing.

CHAPTER TWENTY-SIX
I'm Very Excited

Sunrise on the Reaping would sell 1.5 million copies in the first week after publication. To say that everybody connected to Scholastic was over the moon was obvious. Just how amazing the book did right from the start was quick to be echoed by *The Hollywood Reporter*. Sales were mammoth in the US, UK, Ireland, Canada, Australia and New Zealand. *Sunshine on the Reaping* sold twice as many copies in its first week as *The Ballad of Songbirds and Snakes* and three times as many as *Mockingjay*. *Publisher's Weekly* also reported that the latest Collins' book had rocketed to No. 3 overall in the US bestseller list and was the second biggest debut of the week.

But while being atop the best seller list was a big deal, behind the scenes those connected to bringing the book to the screen had long been preparing for the inevitable *Sunrise of the Reaping: The Movie*, months before the book was published.

The early screenplay team of Danny Strong and Stephen Shields had already been locked in place, along with the ever-present Collins guiding the transition from book to screen. The essentially in-house director of all films in *The Hunger Games* had just completed the long-anticipated sequel to *Constantine*, had celebrated the publication of *Sunrise on the Reaping* on a location scouting trip for the film adaptation that would start later in the year on route to a 2026 movie release.

Producer Nina Jacobson, while celebrating the publication of *Sunrise on the Reaping*, found time to tell *Variety* that the movie had long been uppermost in her mind. "We're very much further along than we would have been otherwise without having this jump because we went to work right away. None of it has been announced yet because we had to wait for the book to be published. But we have a great draft of the script that we're still working on. We've established our locations. We're very far ahead for a book that will not come out until tomorrow. There has been a bit of a challenge in terms of casting because, with the book not yet out, we haven't been able to read for actors."

For director Lawrence, it was very much old home week as he enthusiastically explained in an *Entertainment Tonight* interview. "I read the original manuscript about a year ago and when I read it I fell in love with it. I think that just coming back to a family that we've built and to a world that we've all built, well that's all great. But I think that going back in and telling what I believe is one of her best stories within the franchise is what is really exciting for me

Director Lawrence in another conversation with *Collider.com* echoed the challenges faced with doing much of the prep work on a book that had not yet been published but offered that the production was right on schedule. "We're prepping. We're shooting this year. It's tricky because the book is not yet out. But I am definitely shooting it this year."

Lawrence was enthusiastic at the prospect of bringing *Sunrise on the Reaping* to the screen. "I'm really actually excited for it. *The Hunger Games* is such a great world with great stories and super relevant themes.

Suzanne Collins, The Hunger GamesMaker

"Yeah. I'm very excited."

Well into April 2025, the *Sunrise on the Reaping* continued to play fast and loose with fan expectations and the slightest bit of news. At the *Cinema Con* meeting of theater owners, it was announced that writer Billy Ray was now in charge of putting the final script in place. Ray, who collaborated on the script for the very first *Hunger Games'* movie and went on to an Oscar nomination for his screenplay on the Tom Hanks film *Captain Phillips*, was reported to be the latest piece of the puzzle that Lawrence said had been in the works for a year.

"We've been working on this draft for a year, most of it under lock and key secrecy," he told a *Cinema Con* audience that was hanging on every word. Significant by its absence in the world of speculation was that, as of April 2025, there had still been no official announcement on the casting of the film. But Lawrence was absolutely sure of one thing.

"We will start shooting in July."

Now all that was missing into April 2025 was that little question of a cast. And speculation surrounding just who would be in the cast of *Sunrise on the Reaping* to a large extent, would be just that. *The Express Tribune* would make headlines for a couple of news cycles that, first, actor Ralph Fiennes and, second, Kiefer Sutherland (son of the late actor Donald Sutherland) were being considered to take on the role of Coriolannis Snow. As with most stories of this nature, there would be no confirmation or denial. *Screen Rant.com*, for their part, fanned the fan frenzy when they offered that at least three characters from the original *Hunger Games* trilogy might be making an appearance in the new film.

The longer the legitimate announcement of a cast,

the more rampant the speculation became. *Nexus Point News* was website breathless as it reported that Elle Fanning was set to play the character of Effie Trinket, Charlie Plummer was on board to play Haymitch, Kieran Culkin was in line for the role of Caesar Fleckerman and Emma Thompson was being seriously considered for the latest character addition, Drusilla.

Lawrence for his part, in an interview with *Entertainment Tonight*, would only acknowledge this on the casting question. "We were a little handcuffed because the book wasn't out yet and we were under lockdown with secrets and things like that. But the book is now out and we have full freedom.

"So all I can say is that casting is well underway."

And well under wraps as well. Into April 2025, there was quite a bit of speculation but almost no hint of actual casting announcements. As always, director Lawrence was always seemingly in front of an interviewer, as chronicled in *Woman's Day* when he was asked to speculate on casting the pivotal role of Haymitch Abernathy.

"It's a search and you have to dig down and figure out what are some of the elements that make Woody Harrelson so interesting. Some of it is humor. Some of it is intelligence. Some of it is quirk. There's a darkness to him that gives him an edge. We're going to have to find somebody that has all of that."

Not long after that pronouncement it was announced in outlets such as *People* and *The Wrap.com* that the role had been filled with the casting of actor Joseph Zada. In the same breath it was also announced that actress Whitney Peak was set to play Haymitch's girlfriend Lenore Dove Baird.

The casting of *Sunrise of the Reaping* had finally made it official.

CHAPTER TWENTY-SEVEN
Living the Hunger Games Life

The mania surrounding the publication of *Sunrise on the Reaping* had barely settled when it was replaced by yet another wave of speculation. One that was all too familiar to Collins.

What was next or, perhaps of more immediate scrutiny, what was on tap in the world of *The Hunger Games*?

As of midway through 2025 what was next was a mystery. Not surprisingly, the internet and fandom was ripe with speculation of what might come next. A persistent rumor with a twist was that Collins was finished with *The Hunger Games* and was either about to return to *The Underland Chronicles* or to begin a completely new and different series. Still another offered that a most likely scenario was that there was one more book in *The Hunger Games* prequel set to be announced at any moment.

But there was Scholastic's David Leviathan once again stepping forward to make headlines by being vague in a story that appeared in *Variety*. Leviathan offered that he was not certain what stories Collins wanted to do next but that he felt that she was not going to do another sequel and that he believed the ending of *Mockingjay* was the ending of the series. But Leviathan was not above dancing around the notion of what might be in Collins' head.

"Suzanne always starts with the philosophical point she wants to explore. And I think Haymitch and the *50th Hunger Games* were the perfect grounds on which she could make readers think about the nature of authority and questions of when and when we obey and when we rebel. One of the things about the prequel is that suddenly readers understand that history is made as much by the long game as it is by the immediate battles."

The best that could be offered through websites dedicated to the notion that no news was good news was the dodge that there was no new information about future books in *The Hunger Games* series after *Sunrise on the Reaping* and that neither Collins nor her publisher Scholastic had announced plans for additional *Hunger Games'* books at this time.

Not that there was not ample opportunities to explore *The Hunger Games* universe. The spacing out, time wise, of *The Ballad of Songbirds and Snakes* and *Sunrise on the Reaping* offered literally decades, a massive creative background in which Collins could play. And one thing was certain, *Hunger Games* fans and, on the financial front, Lionsgate, would welcome more *Hunger Games* adventures for years to come.

But who could deny that Suzanne Collins was not entitled to as much time away from the computer screen that she most richly deserved? She had accomplished massive amounts of sweat equity during the life of her creation. Her every written word was eagerly awaited, was critic proof and was sure to be rewarded handsomely.

She had accomplished an amazing feat in the annals of women authors and their fantastic creations, joining the rarified air of the works of J.K. Rowling and Stephanie Meyer.

Suzanne Collins' life and creative times was the dream scenario that most authors would die to have. She had the ability to sell millions of books and to remain, for the most part, a recluse, above such distractions as fandom expectations, public scrutiny and, perhaps most telling, the ability to keep the demands of the publishing and film industry at bay. Collins does not write for profit. She writes for the story and the message she wants to send. But the by product has ultimately been that profit and fame have ultimately found her.

In the best possible way Suzanne Collins was now a brand name whose future on any number of levels was assured. So is there really a rush for more? Not really.

But at her core, Suzanne Collins is a writer who lives by the word and inspiration. So, while the world glories in what she has done, Suzanne Collins may well by finding time to get away from the hysteria and adulation, slipping off to a quiet, alone space, staring into her computer screen, eyes staring, mind working, as her fingers are poised over the keyboard...

Ready to create more magic.

CHAPTER TWENTY-EIGHT
In Her Own Words

Though publicity shy, Suzanne Collins has shared many thoughtful statements about her work, the writing path, and her influences.

"Telling a story in a futuristic world gives you this freedom to explore things that bother you in contemporary times."

* * *

"In *The Hunger Games*, in most people's idea, in terms of rebellion or a civil war situation, that would meet the criteria for a necessary war. These people are oppressed, their children are being taken off and put in gladiator games. They're impoverished. They're starving. They're brutalized."

* * *

"I think people respond to dystopian stories because they're ways of acting out that we have and fears that we have about the future. So much media is coming at you over the internet, your brain gets overloaded, you don't know what to do with it. And one thing you can do with it is read a story."

***

"One of the most memorable things I hear is when someone tells me that my books got a reluctant reader to read."

***

"I don't write about adolescence. I write about war for adolescence."

***

"All the writing elements are the same. You need to tell a good story and you've got to have good characters. People think that there is some dramatic difference between writing *Little Bear* and *The Hunger Games* and, as a writer, for me, there isn't."

***

"Whenever I write a story, I hope it appeals to both boys and girls."

***

"*Lord of the Flies* is one of my favorite books. That book was a big influence on me as a teenager. I still read it every couple of years."

***

"I think it's very uncomfortable for people to talk to children about war so they don't because it's easier not to. But then you have young people at eighteen who are enlisting in the army and they really don't have the slightest idea what they're getting into."

***

"Kids have so much screen time and it's a concern. I know how overloaded I can feel sometime."

* * *

"This is the tenth book so I know certain things that I want to achieve by certain points in the story. If I haven't achieved them, then something isn't working the way I hoped and I probably need to pause and figure out why."

* * *

"The novel *The Ballad of Songbirds and Snakes* began in a philosophical swamp that my brain swam around in until the narrative came to me."

* * *

"When I was young I was trained in stage fighting, raptor and dagger for several years."

* * *

"I try to catch flies in cups and put them outside."

* * *

"I sort of half read Thomas Hardy's *The Mayor of Casterbridge*. It was assigned in the 10th grade and I just couldn't get into it."

* * *

"I'm not a very fancy person."

* * *

"Love can wait. She [Katniss] has a lot of things on her plate. Like staying alive and saving humanity."

* * *

"If you take away the audience, what do you have?"

* * *

"Katniss is not that interested in romance. She equates love and marriage to kids who could be sent to the games."

ADDENDUM:
How The Films Were Made

While Suzanne Collins was given a good portion of the credit in piloting the creative fortunes of *The Hunger Games'* transition from best-selling novels to international top draw movies, she was, with the possible exception of script and casting issues, keeping herself fairly above the fray that was the making of a motion picture. Fortunately for the integrity of the filmmakers, The Hunger Games' movies were uniformly successful and a testament to what team work and just plain hard work can bring to the cinematic table.

THE HUNGER GAMES

In March 2009, Lionsgate Entertainment rolled the dice when they acquired world wide distribution rights to the film version of the novel *The Hunger Games* for a reported $200,000. The studio would soon up the ante when they secured the film rights to the film to be made later for an estimated $88 million. The ever money conscious company quickly knocked down a tax break of major proportions when they announced that the film version of The Hunger Games was to be shot in North Carolina.

A literal list of Hollywood directors immediately lined up to take a shot at what was already being considered an important project, including Gary Ross, Sam Mendes, David Slade. Andrew Adamson, Susanna White, Rupert Sanders and Francis Lawrence. Ross was finally chosen to direct and, as he recalled in *The New York Times*, "I felt the only way to make the film really successful was to have it be totally subjective."

Going in, director Ross had a rather relaxed attitude about how the film should be cast but, ultimately went with Lionsgate's attitude of massive readings and auditions for the two pivotal roles, Katniss Everdeen and Peeta Millark. Consequently, when it came to choosing the actress who would anchor the first and subsequent movies in the series, Collins weighed in with the notion that the role of Katniss "demanded a certain maturity and power.'

Lining up to try their luck were Jennifer Lawrence, Hailee Steinfeld, Abagail Breslin, Emma Roberts, Alyson Stoner, Saoirse Troian, Chole Grace Moretz, Jodelle Ferland, Lyndsy Fonseca, Emily Browning, Shailene Woodly, Kaya Scodelario and Troian Bellisario. The role went to Lawrence.

Joining up for the chance to play Peeta Mallark were Josh Hutcherson, Alexander Ludwig, Hunter Parrish, Lucas Till, Evan Peters and Austin Butler; with the role going to Hutcherson.

The buzz on the film was palpable with countless actors and actresses rushing in to audition. Except for one. Woody Harrelson had been approached to play the strategic character of Haymitch Abernathy but proved initially reluctant to take on the role. But the actor soon changed his mind when director Ross pointed out the

Suzanne Collins, The Hunger GamesMaker

advantage of being in a film that was being hailed as a surefire international hit.

Photography on *The Hunger Games*, initially budgeted at a reported $75 million but ultimately ballooned to an estimated budget of $90 to $100 million, began principal photography in May 11, 2011 near Brevard in Transylvania County in Western North Carolina. One sensed that no expense was being spared when it was revealed that noted director Steven Soderbergh had signed on to direct second unit elements of the film.

A pivotal decision to the creative process was to shoot *The Hunger Games* in film rather than using the digital process. In regards to that decision, director Ross acknowledged in *The New York Times* that "I didn't want to run the risk of the technical issues that often come with shooting digitally. We simply could not afford any delays."

Costume design for the film proved a true creative challenge for head designer Judiahna Makovsky and her team who, as reported by *Vogue* and Glosty.com, looked to 1950's coal mining district photos to get an American feel, the idea being to create clothing unique to every character.

Initially the mood setting score for *The Hunger Games* fell to movie music pros Danny Elfman and T. Bone Burnett. But scheduling conflicts, as detailed by Slash Film.com, Hunger Games Movie.org and Stereogum.org, would resort to the pair departing the project and replaced by the equally talented composer James Newton *Howard.*

The Hunger Games was officially unveiled at the Nokia Theater in Los Angeles on March 12, 2012. The film would commence its official release on March 23, 2012 and received largely positive reviews, most notably for its faithfulness to Collins' book.

Marc Shapiro

THE HUNGER GAMES: CATCHING FIRE

Lionsgate was a firm believer in striking while the iron was hot. The success of *The Hunger Games* box office was freshly in the books when the company announced that principal production on what most perceived was the inevitable sequel, *The Hunger Games: Catching Fire* was to begin in September 2012. This rush to cash in was to have its share of drama.

It had been assumed that director Ross would repeat his duties on *Catching Fire* but he balked at the notion of a tight schedule that, among other issues, would interfere with a previously planned production he was attached to. Then there was the matter of Jennifer Lawrence who, while happy to return to *Catching Fire*, was committed to *X-Men: Days of Future Past*. It was determined that for the actress to do both films, production on *Catching Fire* needed to be finished by December 2012.

The *Catching Fire* production put aside the looming chaos of getting the film off the ground and moved steadily forward. As chronicled in Deadline Hollywood.com, original screenwriter Simon Beaufoy worked on what would be the first two drafts of the script while the likes of Bennett Miller, Joe Cornish, Francis Lawrence and Antonio Bayona jockeyed for favor in the revised race for the *Catching Fire* director's chair.

In the meantime, much credited screenwriter Michael Arndt, as reported in *The Hollywood Reporter*, was brought in to rewrite the existing *Catching Fire* script at the mind-blowing rate of $400,000 a week. Collider was to acknowledge at the time that the musical chairs surrounding actress Lawrence took an unexpected turn when the original director of *X-Men: Days of Future Past* lost its original director and, consequently, Lawrence's services on that film would not be needed for her January 2013 return and thus *Catching Fire* could have Lawrence on set through March 2013.

Secondary roles were quickly filled with Jena Malone portraying Johanna Mason, Amanda Plummer in the role of Wiress, Philip Seymour Hoffman as Plutarch Heavensbee, Lyn Cohen as Mags, Alan Ritcheson as Gloss, Sam Clafin as Finnick Odair and Jeffrey Wright as Beetee.

Filming began on September 12, 2012, by which time everyone connected to their roles were back in a Hunnger Games start of mind. Lawrence, Hutcherson and Hemsworth had dyed their hair back to the first film's color while Lawrence renewed archery training. From the beginning, filming on *The Hunger Games: Catching Fire* was a physical and emotional marathon of six day, 14 hours of shooting at locations in Atlanta, Georgia and Hawaii, By March 2013, the production was centered on the Universal backlot where a series of reportedly secretive sequences was being shot.

Josh Hutcherson, in an MTV interview, acknowledged that much of the film's arena/action sequences had been shot in IMAX, an element of the finished *Catching Fire* that accounted to 50 minutes of the film's running time.

Catching Fire played it safe when it came to the soundtrack for the film with James Newton Howard returning to score the film according to Film Music Reporter.com and the band Coldplay, as reported by Coldplaying.com, returned with another anthem with 'We're A Team.'

Much was expected of *The Hunger Games: Catching Fire* and so nobody was truly surprised when the film opened with a worldwide box office of $865 million according to the outlets Alt Film Guide.com and Box Office Mojo.com and would years later be named the highest grossing film in The Hunger Game series. Needless to say critics were falling all over themselves with praise, for Lawrence's directing skills and the continued exploration of The Hunger Games' further, thought provoking messages.

THE HUNGER GAMES: MOCKINGJAY PART 1

That the novel *The Hunger Games: Mockingjay* was a story of mass complexities and proportions came as no surprise. But, in a sense, it put Lionsgate in a tenuous position. To do Mockingjay as a single, and most likely long film, would mean compromises of massive proportions. Finally in July 2012, after some months of speculation and rumor, Lionsgate announced that they were taking the big chance of splitting the storyline into two separate films to be shot back-to-back and released one year apart.

The likes of Rian Johnson and Alphonso Cuaron were on the short list to direct what had become a massive undertaking. But in the end of the day, Lionsgate decided to play it safe and announced that Francis Lawrence had been confirmed to direct both films. By December 2012, it was further reported that screenwriter Danny Strong would pen both scripts.

According to reports in Deadline Hollywood.com and Hollywood Crush. MTV, casting for secondary roles began in earnest between August and October 2013. Stef Dawson was selected to play Annie Cresta while Julianne Moore was named as Alma Coin. Patina Miller was announced as Commander Paylor, Mahershala Ali as the character of Boggs, Wes Chatham as Castor and Eldon Henson as Pollox.

Suzanne Collins, The Hunger GamesMaker

Filming began on Mockingjay Part 1 on September 23, 2013 in Atlanta, Georgia. Keeping track of which bits of filming were going to end up in which of the two Mockingjay films was not easy. What was known for certain, as reported by IBTtimes.com, The Hunger Games.net and countless other media outlets was that filming in various locations in Georgia wrapped on April 18, 2024 and that the production immediately relocated to Europe where much of the action sequences for both films were filmed in France and Germany.

While the return of James Newton Howard to score the soundtrack of the film seemed a safe and obvious choice, there was moments of creative daring in the process. For several tracks in the film music, the Trinity School Boys Choir was employed. But that paled by comparison when it was announced that Jennifer Lawrence would sing the song 'The Hanging Tree' at a pivotal moment in the film. As chronicled in Entertainment Weekly, the actress was not thrilled at the prospect of singing the song and cried on the day of her performance.

As the day of the November 19, 2014 release of Mockingjay Part 1 drew closer, the speculation of how the first of two parts of the film that would be released a year apart would play was still a sticking point with many observers. Doomsayers insisted that breaking Mockingjay into two films could prove a disjointed exercise that would dilute the impact of The Hunger Games experience.

While there was to be minor grumblings about the lack of action in Part 1, Mockingjay received the expected largely positive reviews that focused on the strength of the storyline and the power and emotion of the message. It came as no real surprise when the film crashed to box office with an initial take of $776 million.

And despite Lawrence's trepidation at singing, 'The Hanging Tree' hit No. 4 on the Apple I Tunes Top 150 List, peaked at No. 1 on the song charts in Austria and Hungary and landed at No. 12 on Billboard's Hot 100 List in the United States.

THE HUNGER GAMES: MOCKINGJAY PART 2

As both Mockingjay films were being shot literally back-to-back, it came as no surprise that things like logistics, budgets and filming schedules tended to overlap. But in the case of Mockingjay Part 2, there was enough of a difference in the process to make things somewhat different and challenging.

Casting Part 2 was eclectic by degrees and very much old home week. Stef Dawson was making a third appearance in the film series as Annie Cresta while Meta Golding made a second film appearance as Enobara. Eugenie Boundarant took on the role of Tigris. And in a bit of stunt casting, twins Misty and Kim were Legg 1 and Legg 2 while Lawrence's Theodore and Bear Lawrence stepped into the roles of Katniss and Peeta's children.

Totally unexpected and sadly tragic was the death of actor Philip Seymour Hoffman in February 2014 during the filming of Part 2. As reported in Variety, Empire Magazine, Cinema Blend.com and The Guardian, Hoffman had already completed his scenes prior to his death but, according to director Lawrence, some changes to subsequent scenes had to be made. "He had two substantial scenes and the rest were appearances in other scenes. We had no intention of trying to fake a performance so we rewrote those scenes and gave the lines to other actors."

The Hunger Games: Mockingjay Part 2 premiered

Suzanne Collins, The Hunger GamesMaker

under a cloud in November 2015 under a continued cloud of speculation because of the novel being split into two films and while it would go on to largely positive reviews and total box office of $661 million, the film was considered a marginal disappointment on all fronts which suggested in many quarters that The Hunger Games films had run their course.

Lionsgate CEO John Feltheimer make well have gotten the hint in a Variety conversation when he suggested that he was interested in having spin offs made of The Hunger Games concept and wanted to create a writer's room to explore the idea. Actress Jennifer Lawrence did not think too much of the idea and suggested as much when she said "I think it's too soon. They've got to let the body get cold first."

THE HUNGER GAMES
THE BALLAD OF SONGBIRDS AND SNAKES

By August 2017, the temperature in The Hunger Games' situation began to warm up. Lionsgate CEO Jon Feltheimer predicted in a Deadline Hollywood story that more Hunger Games stories were most certainly in the pipeline. But he cautiously backtracked when he said that future stories would only come with the approval of Suzanne Collins.

Variety reported in June 2019 that the company was working with Collins on an adaption of The Ballad of Songbirds and Snakes for the big screen.

The big concern in the development of the film version of The Ballad of Songbirds and Snakes was the fact that Collins' novel, much like Mockingjay, was a big book that, from a pure dollars and cents viewpoint, was crying out for two films. But having learned from the backlash of

Mockingjay, it was quickly deduced that one very good version of Collins' story would suffice on the screen.

Casting this film took on an aura of reinventing the wheel with the challenge of essentially adding new faces from top to bottom. Tom Blyth was tabbed for the pivotal role of young President Snow and Rachel Zegler was picked for the role of Lucy Gray Baird. The roles of various tributes and mentors were actors Josh Anders Rivera, Hunter Schafer and Jason Schwartzman while noted actress Viola Davis was selected for the role of Volumina Gaul.

Filming began on July 11, 2022 in the locations in Poland and Germany. The filmmakers, most notably director Lawrence and soundtrack impresario James Newton Howard were, by now, old hands at what made a *Hunger Games* film tick and so *The Ballad of Songbirds and Snakes* was conspicuous by how smooth and stress free the schedule went.

The Ballad of Songbirds and Snakes had its world premiere in November 2023 and would tally a solid early box office of $349 million, good for all intents and purposes but a bit off the box office totals of previous films. Reviews were solid in their praise but there were the expected critical shots when the film was, inevitably, compared to previous offerings, which was expected with this drastic turn in the odyssey. But there was more than enough evidence that justified more to come.

THE HUNGER GAMES
SUNRISE ON THE REAPING

As of May 2025 this is what we know.

The film version of *Sunrise On The Reaping* was announced in June 2024. The script is credited to Billy

Ran and Suzanne Collins. Director Francis Lawrence was in early negotiations to return to the franchise with this film but the consensus was that a deal for him to return was eminent.

According to IMDB.com, the revamped cast includes the following top line roles. Elle Fanning as Effie Trinket, Ralph Fiennes as President Snow, Molly McCann as Loella McCoy, Lili Taylor as Mags Flannagan, Jona Bell as Lou Lou, Maya Hawke as Wiress, Kelvin Harrison Jr. as Beetee Latier, Jesse Plemons as Plutarch Heavensbee, McKenna Grace as Maysilee Donner, Joseph Zada as Haymitch Abernathy, Kieran Culkin as Caesar Flickerman, Ben Wang as Wyatt Callow and Whitney Peak as Lenore Love Baird.

Sunrise On The Reaping is scheduled for a November 20, 2026 release date. Stay tuned. Most certainly more to come.

APPENDIX

SUZANNE COLLINS BIBLIOGRAPHY

THE UNDERLAND CHRONICLES
Gregor The Overlander
(2003)
Gregor and the Prophecy of Bane
(2004)
Gregor and the Curse of the Warmbloods
(2005)
Gregor and the Marks of Secret
2006)

THE HUNGER GAMES
The Hunger Games
(2008)
Catching Fire
(2009)
Mockingjay
(2010)

HUNGER GAMES PREQUELS
The Ballad of Songbirds and Snakes
(2020)
Sunrise on the Reaping
(2025)

Marc Shapiro

OTHER BOOKS
Fire Proof (The Mystery Files of Shelby Woo #11
(1999)
When Charlie McButton Lost Power
(2005)
Year of the Jungle
(2013)

SUZANNE COLLINS FILMOGRAPHY

TELEVISION WRITING CREDITS
Little Bear Rainy Day Tales
(2006)
Children's Christmas Collection
(2006)
Clifford's Puppy Days
(2003-2006)
Wubbzy's Big Movie
(2008)
Wow! Wow! Wubbzy!
(2006-2009)

SCREENWRITING CREDIT
Ticket Out
(2012)
(co-writing credit on direct to video movie)

THE HUNGER GAMES MOVIES
The Hunger Games
(2012)
Director
Gary Ross

Suzanne Collins, The Hunger GamesMaker

Writers
Suzanne Collins, Gary Ross, Billy Ray
Cast
Jennifer Lawrence, Josh Hutcherson, Liam Hemsworth, Stanley Tucci, Wes Bentley, Willow Shields, Elizabeth Banks, Sandra Ellis Lafferty, Paula Malcomson, Rhoda Griffis, Sandra Moya Smith, Raiko Bowman, Dwayne Boyd, Anthony Reynolds, Judd Lormond, Woody Harrelson, Toby Jones, Kimbo Gelman

The Hunger Games: Catching Fire
(2013)
Director
Francis Lawrence
Writers
Suzanne Collins, Simon Beaufoy, Michael Arndt
Cast
Jennifer Lawrence, Josh Hutcherson, Liam Hemsworth, Philip Seymour Hoffman, Jack Quaid, Taylor St. Clair, Sandra Ellis Lafferty, Woody Harrelson, Paula Malcomson, Willow Shields, Donald Sutherland, Elizabeth Banks, Brooke Bundy, Nelson Ascencio, Lenny Kravitz, Stanley Tucci, Afermo Omilami, Kimberly Drummond

The Hunger Games: Mockingjay Part 1
(2014)
Director
Francis Lawrence
Writers
Suzanne Collins, Danny Strong, Peter Craig
Cast
Jennifer Lawrence, Josh Hutcherson,, Liam Hemsworth,

Woody Harrelson, Donald Sutherland, Philip Seymour Hoffman, Julianne Moore, Willow Shields, Sam Clafin, Elizabeth Banks, Mahhersala Ali, Jeria Malone, Jeffrey Wright, Paula Malcomson, Stanley Tucci, Natalie Dorner, Evan Ross, Elden Henson

The Hunger Games: Mockingjay Part 2
(2015)
Director
Francis Lawrence
Writers
Suzanne Collins, Danny Strong, Peter Craig
Cast
Jennifer Lawrence, Josh Hutcherson, Liam Hemsworth, Woody Hemsworth
Woody Harrelson, Donald Sutherland, Philip Seymour Hoffman, Julianne Moore, Willow Shields, Sam Clafin, Elizabeth Banks, Mahersala Ali, Jeria Malone, Jeffrey Wright, Paula Malcomson, Stanley Tucci, Natalie Dorner, Evan Ross, Elden Henson

The Hunger Games:
The Ballad of Songbirds and Snakes
2023)
Director
Francis Lawrence
Writers
Suzanne Collins, Michael Lesslie, Michael Arndt
Cast
Rachel Zegler, Tom Blyth, Viola Davis, Dexter Sol Ansell, Rosa Gottzler, Clemens Schick, Fionnala Flanagan, Hunter Schafer, Ashley Liao, Athena Strates, Joshua Kantara, Amelie Hoeferle, Kaitlyn Akinpelumi,

Suzanne Collins, The Hunger GamesMaker

Florian Burgkart, Ayo Adegun, Aaron Finn Schultz, Max Raphael, Meljus Mulgeta
The Hunger Games: Sunrise of the Reaping
(2026)

AWARDS

THE HUNGER GAMES
(2008)
Cybils Award (won)

(2009)
Locus Award (nominated)
Inky Awards (won)
Golden Duck Award (won)

(2010)
Hampshire Book Awards (won)
Children's Book Awards (won)
Vermont Golden Dome Book Award (won)

(2011)
California Young Reader Medal (won)
Rebecca Caudill Young Readers Book Award (won)
Sequoyah Book Award (won)
Geffen Award (won)

(2012)
Teen Choice Award (won)
Concorde Book Award (won)
Bilby Award (won)

Marc Shapiro

CATCHING FIRE
(2009)
Goodreads Choice Award (won)

(2010)
Golden Duck Award (won)
Locus Award (nominated)
Indies Choice Book Awards (won)

(2012)
Geffen Award (won)

(2014)
Bilby Award (won

(2018)
Goodreads Choice Awards (nominated)

MOCKINGJAY
(2010)
Goodreads Choice Awards (won)

(2011)
Locus Award (nominated)
Andre Norton Award (nominated)

(2013)
Geffen Award (won)

(2016)
Bilby Award (won)

Suzanne Collins, The Hunger GamesMaker

GREGOR AND THE RATS OF UNDERLAND
(2006)
Waterstone's Children's Book Prize (nominated)

YEAR OF THE JUNGLE
(2014)
Christopher Award (won)
Charlotte Zolotow Award (honor)

BOOKS SUZANNE COLLINS LOVES
Myths and Enchanted Tales by Margaret Evans Price
A Wrinkle in Time by Madeleine L' Engle
A Tree Grows in Brooklyn by Betty Smith
1984 by George Orwell
A Moveable Feast by Ernest Hemingway
The Heart is a Lonely Hunter by Carson Mc Cullers
We Have Always Lived in the Castle by Shirley Jackson
Anna Karenina by Leo Tolstoy
Slaughterhouse Five by Kurt Vonnegut
Dandelion Wine by Ray Bradbury
Germinal by Emile Zola
Lord of the Flies by William Golding

SOURCES

MAGAZINES
Time Magazine, Scholastic Magazine, Culturus Magazine, Newsweek, Publishers Weekly, School Library Journal, Entertainment Weekly, People,

BOOKS
The Most Dangerous Cinema: People Hunting People. How to Analyze the Works of Suzanne Collins

NEWSPAPERS
The New York Times, USA Today, Indiana State Student Newspaper, The Sydney Morning Herald, Warsaw Times Union, The Hollywood Reporter, The Guardian, Comic Book Resources, The Plain Dealer, The Los Angeles Times, The Christian Science Monitor, Variety

WEBSITES
The Writing Cooperative.com, AP News.com, World Press.com, AZ Quotes.com, Scholastic Press.com, Mederia 7.com, Brainy Quotes.com, Biography.com, Examiner.com, Book Analysis.com, Puget Sound.com, De Pauw University.edu, Finding Dulicinca.com, Mediaroom. Scholastic.com, Book Page.com, Deseret News.com, Susan Collins Books.com, Sarah Lawrence

Marc Shapiro

Blog, Pop Culture Publishing Media Panel, Scholastic Video.com, Reuters.com, Box Office History Of Lionsgate Movies.com, WGA.com, Suzanne Collins.com, Associated Press.com, PR Newswire.com, CBS News.com, The Wrap.com, IMDB.com, Tick Tock.com, Buzz Feed.com, Yahoo *Entertainment.com, Polygon.com, Screen Rant.com, Dexerto.com, Deadline.com, Den of Geeks.com Living Writer.com, Common Sense Media.com, Booklist.com*

ABOUT THE AUTHOR

New York Times bestselling author Marc Shapiro has written more than 60 nonfiction celebrity biographies, more than 24 comic books, numerous short stories and poetry, and three short-form screenplays. He is also a veteran freelance entertainment journalist.

His young adult book, *JK Rowling: The Wizard Behind Harry Potter,* was on *The New York Times* bestseller list for four straight weeks. His fact-based book *Total Titanic* was also on *The Los Angeles Times* bestseller list for four weeks. *Justin Bieber: The Fever* was on the nationwide Canadian bestseller list for several weeks. *Behind Sad Eyes: The Life of George Harrison* was on *The London Times* Bestseller list.

Shapiro has written books on such personalities as Shonda Rhimes, George Harrison, Carlos Santana, Annette Funicello, Lorde, Lindsay Lohan, E.L. James, Jamie Dornan, Dakota Johnson, Adele and countless others. He also co-authored the autobiography of mixed martial arts fighter Tito Ortiz, *This is Gonna Hurt: The Life of a Mixed Martial Arts Champion.*

He is currently working on a musical biography of the rock group Oasis and the group biography *Beatle Kids* for Riverdale Avenue Books.

Other Riverdale Avenue Books Titles by Marc Shapiro

Beatle Wives:
The Women the Men We Loved Fell in Love With

Word Up: The Life of Amanda Gorman

Keanu Reeves' Excellent Adventure
An Unofficial Biography

Hard Work: The Greta Van Fleet Story

Lorde: Your Heroine, How This Young Feminist
Broke the Rules and Succeeded

Legally Bieber: Justin Bieber at 18

You're Gonna Make It After All:
The Life, Times and Influence of Mary Tyler Moore

Hey Joe:
The Unauthorized Biography of a Rock Classic

What is Hip?
The Life and Times of the Tragically Hip

Marc Shapiro

***Trump This! The Life and Times of Donald Trump,
An Unauthorized Biography***

The Secret Life of EL James

***The Real Steele:
The Unauthorized Biography of Dakota Johnson***

***Inside Grey's Anatomy:
The Unauthorized Biography of Jamie Dornan***

Annette Funicello: America's Sweetheart

Game: The Resurrection of Tim Tebow

***Lindsay Lohan: Fully Loaded,
From Disney to Disaster***

We Love Jenni: An Unauthorized Biography

Who Is Katie Holmes? An Unauthorized Biography

***Norman Reedus: True Tales of
The Waking Dead's Zombie Hunter,
An Unauthorized Biography***

***Welcome to Shondaland:
An Unauthorized Biography of Shonda Rhimes***

Renaissance Man: The Lin Manuel Story

John McCain: View from the Hill

www.ingramcontent.com/pod-product-compliance
Lightning Source LLC
Chambersburg PA
CBHW070159100426
42743CB00013B/2974